Ernst Schubert

Tables of Parthenope

Ernst Schubert

Tables of Parthenope

ISBN/EAN: 9783743330177

Manufactured in Europe, USA, Canada, Australia, Japa

Cover: Foto ©ninafisch / pixelio.de

Manufactured and distributed by brebook publishing software
(www.brebook.com)

Ernst Schubert

Tables of Parthenope

TABLES

OF

PARTHENOPE,

BY

E. SCHUBERT.

COMPUTED FOR THE

AMERICAN EPHEMERIS AND NAUTICAL ALMANAC.

BUREAU OF NAVIGATION,
WASHINGTON.
1871.

INTRODUCTION.

IN the construction of these Tables some twenty of the smaller terms of the perturbations by Jupiter and Saturn, published in No. 1761 of the "Astronomische Nachrichten," have been omitted, since the effect of them upon the final result is almost everywhere nearly zero.

Denoting the arguments in the following manner:—

I $=$	$- M'$	XI $=$	$- M''$	XXI $=$	$3 M - 4 M'$
II $=$	$2 M - 3 M'$	XII $=$	$M - M''$	XXII $=$	$2 M - 5 M'$
III $=$	$M - 3 M'$	XIII $=$	$2 M - M''$	XXIII $=$	$M - 6 M'$
IV $=$	$M - M'$	XIV $=$	$M - 2 M''$	XXIV $=$	$3 M - 5 M'$
V $=$	$M - 2 M'$	XV $= -$	$M - 3 M'$	XXV $=$	$4 M - 5 M'$
VI $=$	$2 M - M'$	XVI $=$	$4 M - 3 M'$	XXVI $=$	$M - 5 M'$
VII $=$	$3 M - 2 M'$	XVII $= -$	$2 M - 3 M'$	XXVII $= -2 M - M'$	
VIII $= - M -$	M'	XVIII $= -$	$M - 2 M'$	XXVIII $=$	$5 M - 2 M'$
IX $=$	M	XIX $=$	$M - 4 M'$	XXIX $=$	$4 M - M'$
X $=$	$3 M - M'$	XX $=$	$5 M - 3 M'$	XXX $= - M - M''$	

The perturbations by Jupiter and Saturn, retained for the construction of the Tables, in units of the sixth decimal are:—

	ξ_i		η_i		ζ_i	
	cos	sin	cos	sin	cos	sin
0 M .	$- 16.08t$		$- 134.23t$		$+ 4.22t$	
1 M	$- 0.75t$	$+ 69.97t$	$- 87.87t$	$- 1.33t$	$- 28.27t$	$+ 0.79t$
2 M	$+ 5.25t$	$+ 51.69t$	$- 51.92t$	$+ 5.23t$	$- 1.40t$	$+ 0.04t$
3 M	$+ 0.78t$	$+ 7.72t$	$- 7.44t$	$+ 0.78t$	$- 0.10t$	
4 M	$+ 0.10t$	$+ 0.96t$	$- 0.96t$	$+ 0.10t$	$- 0.01t$	
5 M	$+ 0.01t$	$+ 0.12t$	$- 0.11t$	$+ 0.01t$		
I	$+ 607.1$	$+ 924.2$	$+ 933.1$	$- 600.5$	$+ 20.6$	$- 14.8$
2 I	$+ 694.5$	$- 1272.7$	$- 1269.2$	$- 690.7$	$- 15.3$	$- 12.3$
3 I	-3832.4	-15443.2	-15398.8	$+3818.4$	$- 27.3$	$+ 11.5$
4 I	$+ 1.1$	$- 10.8$	$- 10.8$	$- 1.1$		
5 I	0.0	$- 2.3$	$- 2.3$	0.0		
6 I	$+ 1.4$	$+ 6.7$	$+ 6.7$	$- 1.3$		
II	$+3682.2$	$+14639.1$	-14575.4	$+3198.5$	$- 63.8$	$- 342.7$
2 II	$+ 16.3$	$- 11.0$	$+ 17.0$	$+ 7.2$		
III	-3783.1	$- 3604.8$	$- 3648.8$	$+3783.2$	$+ 18.4$	$+ 45.3$
2 III	$- 41.8$	$+ 23.4$	$+ 25.1$	$+ 30.9$		

	ξ_i		η_i		ζ_i	
	cos	sin	cos	sin	cos	sin
IV	+ 29.9	− 108.6	+ 124.0	+ 31.6	− 3.0	+ 7.7
2 IV	− 434.5	+ 774.0	− 739.0	− 412.4	+ 4.5	− 0.9
3 IV	+1576.5	+2644.5	−2641.9	+1568.3	− 2.7	− 17.3
4 IV	− 7.0	+ 18.9	− 17.7	− 10.2		
5 IV	− 0.7	+ 2.5	− 0.9	− 1.1		
V	+ 620.1	−1521.7	−1532.5	− 555.5	+ 38.5	+ 17.5
2 V	+ 24.3	− 67.9	− 87.3	− 5.5	+ 8.5	+ 4.0
3 V	+ 4.0	− 66.7	+ 55.3	+ 2.6	− 4.9	− 1.2
4 V	− 1.3		− 0.5			
VI	− 280.9	− 444.6	+ 442.2	− 279.2	+ 9.0	− 6.3
2 VI	− 29.7	+ 73.6	− 73.4	− 29.6		
3 VI	+ 2.8	+ 5.2	− 5.2	+ 2.8		
VII	− 195.3	+ 466.6	− 464.5	− 194.5	+ 2.6	+ 0.8
2 VII	− 0.9			− 0.9		
VIII	+ 24.6	+ 152.2	+ 151.6	− 24.9	+ 7.9	− 0.6
2 VIII	+ 3.5	− 10.8	− 10.8	− 3.5		
3 VIII	− 4.5	− 19.3	− 19.2	+ 4.6		
0 IX	− 3.8		+ 10.7		+ 1.1	
1 IX	+ 170.0	− 0.6	− 1.0	+ 159.7		+ 0.1
2 IX	+ 16.4	− 7.1	+ 7.0	+ 16.3		+ 1.4
3 IX		− 0.9	+ 0.9			
X	− 37.1	− 61.7	+ 61.5	− 37.0		
2 X	− 0.5	+ 1.2	− 1.2	− 0.5		
XI	− 29.8	+ 29.5	+ 33.2	+ 35.7		
2 XI		+ 48.2	+ 48.2			
3 XI	+ 2.5	+ 13.0	+ 13.0	− 2.9		
XII	+ 3.8	+ 9.0	− 10.6	+ 2.8		
2 XII		− 19.9	+ 20.0			
3 XII	0.8	− 2.5	+ 2.5	− 0.7		
XIII	+ 12.8	− 11.1	+ 11.0	+ 12.8		
2 XIII		− 1.1	+ 1.1			
XIV	+ 4.3	+ 22.1	+ 23.1	+ 1.7		
2 XIV	− 0.9	− 0.6		+ 0.8		
XV	− 368.2	−1501.3	−1499.5	+ 367.3	1.4	+ 0.6
XVI	+ 196.2	+ 346.7	− 346.6	+ 195.8		
XVII	− 40.6	− 166.2	− 166.0	+ 40.5		
XVIII	+ 39.7	− 105.2	− 105.2	− 39.8	− 0.8	− 1.0

	ξ_1		η_1		ζ_1	
	cos	sin	cos	sin	cos	sin
XIX	+101.9	− 59.8	− 62.3	−100.0	− 1.8	− 1.3
XX	+ 22.4	+ 42.4	− 42.0	+ 22.1		
XXI	− 13.3	+ 52.7	+ 1.4	− 73.2	+ 4.3	− 4.0
XXII	− 26.2	− 15.6	− 17.9	+ 25.7		
XXIII	− 5.7	+ 67.9	+ 67.4	+ 6.7		
XXIV	+ 16.6	+ 7.2	− 19.8	− 17.0	− 0.9	− 3.5
XXV	+ 5.4	+ 16.7	+ 5.4	+ 7.4	+ 1.1	
XXVI	− 1.0	− 22.8	− 22.8	+ 1.1		
XXVII	+ 1.3	+ 16.8	+ 16.9	− 1.2		
XXVIII	− 4.0	+ 10.2	− 9.9	− 3.9		
XXIX	− 4.7	− 7.8	+ 7.9	− 4.7		
XXX	− 5.3	− 6.1	− 5.9	+ 5.4		

Normals referred to the mean equinox 1850.0.

Berlin M. T.		a	δ	Berlin M. T.	a	δ
1850 May	31.0	225° 57′ 33″.5	− 9° 44′ 27″.9	1859 December	2.0	67° 40′ 6″.8	+15° 31′ 7″.3
1851 October	22.0	28 46 48.3	+ 3 20 40.6	1861 March	13.0	172 44 43.7	+ 8 55 54.5
1853 February	7.0	141 50 9.9	+16 50 37.7	1862 July	26.0	306 21 31.2	−19 3 26.1
1854 June	3.0	252 46 36.7	−16 0 53.0	1863 December	8.0	88 56 39.5	+18 36 38.2
1855 November	9.0	49 49 12.4	+10 32 47.2	1865 March	28.0	189 4 52.7	+ 3 18 58.3
1857 February	20.0	158 10 19.5	+12 58 7.7	1866 August	24.0	334 30 24.6	−14 35 2.7
1858 June	18.0	281 16 13.4	−18 50 29.8	1868 January	3.0	103 56 14.8	+20 3 8.3

Elements.

1850, Jan. 0, Washington Mean Time.

$$M = 250°\ 52'\ 17''.3 \qquad \varphi = 5°\ 45'\ 40''.4$$
$$\pi = 316\ 46\ 46.3 \left.\right\} \text{M. Eq. Ep.} \qquad \mu = 923''.8703$$
$$\Omega = 124\ 58\ 43.9 \qquad \log a = 0.389597$$
$$i = 4\ 37\ 32.1$$

Example for computing a Place from the Tables.

1870, September 20.5, Berlin M. T. = September 20, $5^h\ 58^m\ 15^s$ Washington M. T.

In the first place we have to write down the constants to be used :—

	$\log e$		$\log \frac{1-e}{1+e}$		$\log p$	
From Table II.,	9.001660		9.912513		0.385199	
	$\cos(x_1\,x)$	$\cos(y_1\,x)$	$\cos(z_1\,x)$	$\cos(x_1\,y)$	$\cos(y_1\,y)$	
From Table V.,	9.861213	9.831649	8.818516	9.791508n	9.845887	
	$\cos(z_1\,y)$	$\cos(x_1\,z)$	$\cos(y_1\,z)$	$\cos(z_1\,z)$		
	9.549111n	9.457092n	9.339004	9.969831		

	A'	B'	C'	log sin a	log sin b	log sin c

And from Table VI., $47\ 8\ 45.9$ $318\ 31\ 39.4$ $307\ 18\ 16.4$ 9.999056 9.970910 9.556492

M = mean anomaly ; t = time since 1850.0.

From Table I., M t

1870	$325\ 33\ 29.84$	$+20.0000$
September	$62\ 21\ 40.48$	0.6653
20 days	$5\ 7\ 57.40$	0.0518
5 hours	$3\ 12.47$	0.0006
58 minutes	37.21	
15 seconds	0.16	
	$33\ 6\ 57.56$	$+20.7207$

$$\cot \tfrac{1}{2} M \qquad 16\ 33\ 28.8 \qquad 0.526783$$
$$\frac{1-e}{1+e}\cot \tfrac{1}{2} M = \cot \tfrac{1}{2} v' \qquad 19\ 59\ 4.8 \qquad 0.439296$$
$$v' \qquad 39\ 58\ 9.6$$

From Table II. $\quad c+\qquad 16\ 51.6$

$$v \qquad 40\ 7\ 1.2$$
$$\cos v \qquad\qquad 9.883508$$
$$e \cos v \qquad +0.076766 \qquad 8.885168$$
$$1 + e \cos v \qquad 1.076766 \qquad 0.032121$$
$$r \qquad\qquad 0.353078$$

Formation of the Arguments from Table III.*

	I.	II.	III.	IV.	V.	VI.	VII.	VIII.	IX.	X.
1870	324.734	185.318	219.760	290.292	455.03	255.85	186.14	359.17	325.56	291.41
September . .	339.814	64.152	1.796	42.158	21.99	104.54	146.70	277.45	62.34	166.89
20 days . . .	358.338	5.280	0.148	3.470	1.81	8.60	12.07	353.20	5.13	13.74
6 hours . . .	359.979	0.066	0.002	0.043	0.02	0.11	0.15	359.92	6.06	0.17
	302.865	254.816	221.706	335.963	278.85	9.10	345.06	269.74	33.09	42.21

	XI.	XII.	XIII.	XIV.	XV.	XVI.	XVII.	XVIII.	XIX.	XX.
1870	191.6	157.2	122.8	348.8	288.6	116.4	323.1	323.9	184.5	82.0
September . .	351.9	54.2	116.6	46.1	237.0	188.9	174.7	257.2	341.6	251.2
20 days . .	359.3	4.5	9.6	3.8	349.9	15.5	344.8	351.6	358.5	20.7
	182.8	215.9	249.0	38.7	155.5	320.8	122.6	212.7	164.6	353.9

	XXI.	XXII.	XXIII.	XXIV.	XXV.	XXVI.	XXVII.	XXVIII.	XXIX.	XXX.
1870	116	115	114	80	46	149	34	117	187	296
September . .	106	24	301	86	148	321	215	271	229	289
20 days . . .	9	2	355	7	12	357	348	22	19	354
	231	141	50	173	206	107	237	50	75	149

* The arguments being expressed in degrees and decimals, 360.0, 720.0, or 1080.0 must be subtracted when one of the sums is greater than one of those numbers.

Terms	ξ' +	ξ' −	η' +	η' −	ζ' +	ζ' −
Terms with t	1632.8	−	+	4372.1	+	404.5
I	6515.5	15112.1	16899.6		66.3	
II			718.2		347.5	
III	5241.2		237.5			44.0
IV		2851.1		2379.5	13.4	
V	1533.8		375.5			19.3
VI		347.5	310.8		7.7	
VII		308.0		399.3		
VIII		175.0	39.4			
IX	137.3		114.7		7.2	
X		67.6	20.0			
XI	28.8		0.4			
XII		25.0	14.4			
XIII	5.0		16.6			
XIV	16.4		19.8			
XV		248.3	1513.8		1.5	
XVI		65.7		392.3		
XVII		119.0	122.7			
XVIII	23.9		109.7		1.2	
XIX		113.5	34.1		1.4	
XX	17.9			44.0		
XXI		32.6	56.0			
XXII	10.0		30.2			
XXIII	49.3		48.4			
XXIV		15.6	17.9			
XXV		12.4		8.2		
XXVI		21.5	7.7			
XXVII		12.8		8.1		
XXVIII	5.6			9.0		
XXIX		8.6		2.6		
XXX	1.5			7.6		
	15218.0	19576.3	20645.0	7615.1	446.2	467.8
ξ', η', ζ'	−4358.3		+13029.9		−21.6	

Right-hand section:

$\cos(x_1 x)\,\xi'$	− 3188.2	
$\cos(y_1 x)\,\eta'$	+ 8942.8	
$\cos(z_1 x)\,\zeta'$	− 1.4	
ξ	+ 5653.2	
$\cos(x_1 y)\,\xi'$	+ 2606.7	
$\cos(y_1 y)\,\eta'$	+ 9137.5	
$\cos(z_1 y)\,\zeta'$	+ 7.6	
η	+11841.8	
$\cos(x_1 z)\,\xi'$	+ 1248.6	
$\cos(y_1 z)\,\eta'$	+ 2844.1	
$\cos(z_1 z)\,\zeta'$	− 20.2	
ζ	+ 4072.5	
$\sin(A' + \tau)$	87 15 47.1	9.999505
$r \sin a$		0.352134
z		0.351639
$\sin(B' + \tau)$	358 41 40.6	8.357580n
$r \sin b$		0.323988
y		8.681568n
$\sin(C' + \tau)$	347 25 17.6	9.338011n
$r \sin c$		9.909570
z		9.247581n
y	− 0.048036	
η	+ 11842	
Y	+ 0.036089	
$\Delta \cos \delta' \sin a'$	− 0.000105	6.021189n
x	+ 2.247185	
ξ	+ 5653	
X	− 1.002746	
$\Delta \cos \delta' \cos a'$	+ 1.250092	0.006942
$\cos a'$		0.000000
$\tan a'$	359 59 42.7	5.924247n
z	− 0.176840	
ζ	+ 4072	
Z	+ 0.015661	
$\Delta \sin \delta'$	− 0.157107	9.196196n
$\Delta \cos \delta'$		0.006942
$\cos \delta'$		9.996597
$\tan \delta'$	− 7 9 47.4	9.099254n
Δ		0.100345

a' and δ' are referred to the mean equinox 1870.0

Reduction to the apparent equinox.

$$f \quad + 17.88$$
$$g \quad 0.9036$$
$$G \quad 13\ 9$$
$$\sin(G + a') \quad 13\ 9 \quad 9.3570$$
$$\tan \delta' \quad 9.0993n$$
$$- 0.23 \quad 9.3599$$
$$\Delta a' \quad + 17.65$$
$$\cos(G + a') \quad 9.9885$$
$$\Delta \delta' \quad + 7.80 \quad 0.8921$$
$$a = 3\ 6\ 0.3$$
$$\delta = -7\ 9\ 30.6$$

TABLE I.
FOR THE MEAN ANOMALY.
For Washington mean noon of Jan. 0 in common years, of Jan. 1 in bissextile years.

Years.	M	t	Years.	M	t
1850	258 52 17.30	0.0000	1876 *D*	168 5 33.54	+26.0014
1851	344 32 20.96	+ 0.9993	1877	261 45 46.20	27.0007
1852 *B*	78 23 6.49	2.0014	1878	355 25 58.86	28.0000
1853	172 8 19.15	3.0007	1879	89 6 11.52	28.9993
1854	265 49 31.81	4.0000	1880 *B*	183 1 48.05	30.0014
1855	359 29 44.47	4.9993	1881	276 42 0.71	31.0007
1856 *B*	93 24 21.00	6.0014	1882	10 22 13.37	32.0000
1857	187 4 33.66	7.0007	1883	104 2 26.03	32.9993
1858	280 44 46.32	8.0000	1884 *B*	197 58 2.56	34.0014
1859	14 24 58.98	8.9993	1885	291 39 15.22	35.0007
1860 *B*	108 20 35.51	10.0014	1886	25 18 27.88	36.0000
1861	202 0 48.17	11.0007	1887	118 58 40.53	36.9993
1862	295 41 0.82	12.0000	1888 *B*	212 54 17.06	38.0014
1863	29 21 13.48	12.9993	1889	306 34 29.72	39.0007
1864 *B*	123 16 50.01	14.0014	1890	40 14 42.38	40.0000
1865	216 57 2.67	15.0007	1891	133 54 56.04	40.9993
1866	310 37 15.33	16.0000	1892 *B*	227 50 31.57	42.0014
1867	44 17 28.00	16.9993	1893	321 30 44.23	43.0007
1868 *B*	138 13 4.52	18.0014	1894	55 10 56.89	44.0000
1869	231 53 17.18	19.0007	1895	148 51 9.55	44.9993
1870	325 33 29.84	20.0000	1896 *B*	242 46 46.08	46.0014
1871	59 13 42.50	20.9993	1897	336 26 58.74	47.0007
1872 *B*	153 9 19.03	22.0014	1898	70 7 11.40	48.0000
1873	246 49 31.69	23.0007	1899	163 47 24.06	48.9993
1874	340 29 44.35	24.0000	1900 *B*	257 43 0.59	+50.0014
1875	74 9 57.01	+24.9993			

Months.	M	t	Days.	M	t
January	8 6 0.00	0.0000	1	8 15 23.87	+ 0.0027
February	7 57 19.98	+ 0.0849	2	0 30 47.74	0.0055
March	15 8 28.35	0.1615	3	0 46 11.61	0.0082
April	23 5 48.33	0.2464	4	1 1 35.48	0.0109
May	30 47 44.44	0.3286	5	1 16 59.35	0.0137
June	38 45 4.41	0.4134	6	1 32 23.22	0.0164
July	46 27 0.52	0.4956	7	1 47 47.09	0.0192
August	54 24 20.50	0.5805	8	2 3 10.96	0.0219
September	62 21 40.48	0.6653	9	2 18 34.83	0.0246
October	70 3 36.59	0.7475	10	2 33 58.70	0.0274
November	78 0 56.57	0.8324	20	5 7 57.40	0.0548
December	85 42 52.68	+ 0.9145	30	7 41 56.10	+ 0.0821

In Bissextile Years one day must be subtracted from the date in the first two months.

TABLE I.—*Concluded.*

FOR THE MEAN ANOMALY.

The times are referred to the meridian of Washington.

Hours.	M	t	Hours.	M	t
	′ ″			′ ″	
1	0 38.49	+0.0001	13	8 20.43	+0.0015
2	1 16.99	0.0002	14	8 58.92	0.0016
3	1 55.48	0.0003	15	9 37.42	0.0017
4	2 33.98	0.0005	16	10 15.91	0.0018
5	3 12.47	0.0006	17	10 54.41	0.0019
6	3 50.97	0.0007	18	11 32.90	0.0021
7	4 29.46	0.0008	19	12 11.40	0.0022
8	5 7.96	0.0009	20	12 49.89	0.0023
9	5 46.45	0.0010	21	13 28.39	0.0024
10	6 24.94	0.0011	22	14 6.88	0.0025
11	7 3.44	0.0013	23	14 45.37	0.0026
12	7 41.93	+0.0014	24	15 23.87	+0.0027

	M			M	
	For Minutes.	For Seconds.		For Minutes.	For Seconds.
	′	″		′	″
1	0.64	0.01	31	19.89	0.33
2	1.28	0.02	32	20.53	0.34
3	1.92	0.03	33	21.17	0.35
4	2.57	0.04	34	21.81	0.36
5	3.21	0.05	35	22.45	0.37
6	3.85	0.06	36	23.10	0.38
7	4.49	0.07	37	23.74	0.40
8	5.13	0.09	38	24.38	0.41
9	5.77	0.10	39	25.02	0.42
10	6.42	0.11	40	25.66	0.43
11	7.06	0.12	41	26.30	0.44
12	7.70	0.13	42	26.95	0.45
13	8.34	0.14	43	27.59	0.46
14	8.98	0.15	44	28.23	0.47
15	9.62	0.16	45	28.87	0.48
16	10.27	0.17	46	29.51	0.49
17	10.91	0.18	47	30.15	0.50
18	11.55	0.19	48	30.80	0.51
19	12.19	0.20	49	31.44	0.52
20	12.83	0.21	50	32.08	0.53
21	13.47	0.22	51	32.72	0.55
22	14.11	0.24	52	33.36	0.56
23	14.76	0.25	53	34.00	0.57
24	15.40	0.26	54	34.64	0.58
25	16.04	0.27	55	35.29	0.59
26	16.68	0.28	56	35.93	0.60
27	17.32	0.29	57	36.57	0.61
28	17.96	0.30	58	37.21	0.62
29	18.61	0.31	59	37.85	0.63
30	19.25	0.32	60	38.49	0.64

TABLE II.

FOR THE CORRECTION c TO BE ADDED TO THE AUXILIARY ANOMALY v'.

Argument = M. For M > 180° the Argument is 360° − M, and the sign of c to be reversed.

Arg.	c	Diff.	Arg.	c	Diff.	Arg.	c	Diff.	Arg.	c	Diff.	Arg.	c	Diff.
0	0 0.0		45	+8 52.2	−5.1	90	−2 16.3	−16.9	135	−8 7.4	+3.3			
1	+0 22.3	+22.3	46	8 47.1	5.8	91	2 33.2	16.6	136	8 4.1	3.8			
2	0 44.6	22.3	47	8 41.3	6.6	92	2 49.8	16.3	137	8 0.3	4.2			
3	1 6.9	22.3	48	8 34.7	7.3	93	3 6.1	16.1	138	7 56.1	4.7			
4	1 29.0	22.1	49	8 27.4	8.0	94	3 22.2	15.7	139	7 51.4	5.1			
5	1 50.9	21.9	50	8 19.4	8.7	95	3 37.9	15.4	140	7 46.3	5.6			
6	2 12.7	21.8	51	8 10.7	9.4	96	3 53.3	15.1	141	7 40.7	6.0			
7	2 34.2	21.5	52	8 1.3	10.0	97	4 8.4	14.8	142	7 34.7	6.4			
8	2 55.5	21.3	53	7 51.3	10.6	98	4 23.2	14.3	143	7 28.3	6.9			
9	3 16.5	21.0	54	7 40.7	11.3	99	4 37.5	14.0	144	7 21.4	7.3			
10	3 37.1	20.6	55	7 29.4	11.8	100	4 51.5	13.7	145	7 14.1	7.7			
11	3 57.3	20.2	56	7 17.6	12.4	101	5 5.2	13.2	146	7 6.4	8.0			
12	4 17.1	19.8	57	7 5.2	12.9	102	5 18.4	12.8	147	6 58.4	8.5			
13	4 36.5	19.4	58	6 52.3	13.4	103	5 31.2	12.3	148	6 49.9	8.8			
14	4 55.4	18.9	59	6 38.9	13.9	104	5 43.5	12.0	149	6 41.1	9.2			
15	5 13.9	18.5	60	6 25.0	14.4	105	5 55.5	11.5	150	6 31.9	9.6			
16	5 31.8	17.9	61	6 10.6	14.9	106	6 7.0	11.0	151	6 22.3	9.9			
17	5 49.1	17.3	62	5 55.7	15.2	107	6 18.0	10.6	152	6 12.4	10.2			
18	6 5.8	16.7	63	5 40.5	15.6	108	6 28.6	10.2	153	6 2.2	10.6			
19	6 21.9	16.1	64	5 24.9	16.0	109	6 38.8	9.6	154	5 51.6	10.8			
20	6 37.3	15.4	65	5 8.9	16.4	110	6 48.4	9.2	155	5 40.8	11.2			
21	6 52.1	14.8	66	4 52.5	16.8	111	6 57.6	8.7	156	5 29.6	11.5			
22	7 6.2	14.1	67	4 35.9	16.9	112	7 6.3	8.2	157	5 18.1	11.7			
23	7 19.6	13.4	68	4 19.0	17.2	113	7 14.5	7.7	158	5 6.4	12.1			
24	7 32.3	12.7	69	4 1.8	17.5	114	7 22.2	7.2	159	4 54.3	12.3			
25	7 44.2	11.9	70	3 44.3	17.6	115	7 29.4	6.7	160	4 42.0	12.5			
26	7 55.3	11.1	71	3 26.7	17.9	116	7 36.1	6.3	161	4 29.5	12.8			
27	8 5.7	10.4	72	3 8.8	18.0	117	7 42.4	5.7	162	4 16.7	13.0			
28	8 15.3	9.6	73	2 50.8	18.1	118	7 48.1	5.2	163	4 3.7	13.2			
29	8 24.1	8.8	74	2 32.7	18.2	119	7 53.3	4.7	164	3 50.5	13.4			
30	8 32.0	7.9	75	2 14.5	18.4	120	7 58.0	4.1	165	3 37.1	13.6			
31	8 39.2	7.2	76	1 56.1	18.3	121	8 2.1	3.7	166	3 23.5	13.8			
32	8 45.5	6.3	77	1 37.8	18.5	122	8 5.8	3.1	167	3 9.7	13.8			
33	8 51.0	5.5	78	1 19.3	18.4	123	8 8.9	2.7	168	2 55.7	14.0			
34	8 55.6	4.6	79	1 0.9	18.4	124	8 11.6	2.1	169	2 41.6	14.1			
35	8 59.5	3.9	80	0 42.5	18.4	125	8 13.7	1.6	170	2 27.4	14.2			
36	9 2.5	3.0	81	0 24.1	18.4	126	8 15.3	1.1	171	2 13.0	14.4			
37	9 4.6	2.1	82	+0 5.7	18.2	127	8 16.4	0.6	172	1 58.5	14.5			
38	9 5.9	1.3	83	−0 12.5	18.2	128	8 17.0	−0.2	173	1 43.9	14.6			
39	9 6.4	+0.5	84	0 30.6	18.1	129	8 17.2	+0.4	174	1 29.3	14.6			
40	9 6.0	−0.4	85	0 48.7	18.1	130	8 16.8	0.9	175	1 14.5	14.8			
41	9 4.9	1.1	86	1 6.6	17.9	131	8 15.9	1.4	176	0 59.7	14.8			
42	9 2.9	2.0	87	1 24.3	17.7	132	8 14.5	1.8	177	0 44.8	14.9			
43	9 0.1	2.8	88	1 41.8	17.5	133	8 12.6	2.3	178	0 29.9	14.9			
44	8 56.6	3.5	89	1 59.2	17.4	134	8 10.3	+2.9	179	−0 14.9	15.0			
45	8 52.2	−4.4	90	−2 16.3	17.1	135	−8 7.4		180	0 0.0	+14.9			

$$\cot \tfrac{1}{2} v' = \frac{1-e}{1+e} \cos \tfrac{1}{2} M$$

$$r = \frac{p}{1+e \cos v}$$

True Anomaly $r = r' + c$

$$\log \frac{1-e}{1+e} = 9.919513$$

$$\log p = 0.385199 \qquad \log e = 9.001660$$

TABLE III.

FOR THE ARGUMENTS.

A. For the different Years. The times are referred to the meridian of Washington.

Years.	I.	II.	III.	IV.	V.	VI.	VII.	VIII.	IX.	X.
1850	211.657	56.713	165.842	102.528	314.18	353.40	95.93	320.79	250.87	244.27
1851	181.332	153.080	168.538	165.874	347.21	150.42	316.29	196.79	314.54	134.96
1852 B	150.924	249.708	171.240	229.392	20.32	307.86	177.25	72.46	78.47	26.33
1853	120.508	346.072	173.933	292.737	53.33	104.88	37.61	308.46	172.14	277.01
1854	90.273	82.437	176.628	356.082	86.35	261.89	257.97	184.46	265.81	167.70
1855	59.947	178.799	179.320	59.426	119.37	58.90	118.33	60.47	359.48	58.34
1856 B	29.539	275.429	182.023	122.945	152.48	216.35	359.30	296.13	93.41	309.76
1857	359.213	11.791	184.715	186.289	185.50	13.36	199.65	172.14	187.08	200.44
1858	328.888	108.156	187.410	249.634	218.52	170.38	60.01	48.14	280.75	91.13
1859	298.562	204.518	190.102	312.978	251.54	327.39	240.37	284.15	14.42	341.81
1860 B	268.154	301.148	192.805	16.497	284.65	124.84	141.231	159.81	108.34	233.18
1861	237.824	37.511	195.497	79.811	317.67	281.85	1.69	35.81	202.01	123.87
1862	207.503	133.876	198.193	143.187	350.69	78.87	222.06	271.82	295.69	14.55
1863	177.178	230.212	200.888	206.532	23.71	235.89	82.42	147.82	29.35	265.24
1864 B	146.769	326.869	203.588	270.050	56.82	33.33	303.38	23.49	123.28	156.61
1865	116.444	63.234	206.289	333.395	89.84	190.35	163.74	259.49	216.95	47.30
1866	86.119	159.599	208.978	36.740	122.86	347.36	24.10	135.50	310.62	297.98
1867	55.793	255.961	211.670	100.084	155.88	141.37	244.46	11.50	44.99	188.67
1868 B	25.385	352.591	214.373	163.603	188.99	301.82	105.42	247.17	138.22	80.04
1869	355.060	88.956	217.068	226.948	222.01	98.81	325.78	123.17	231.80	330.72
1870	324.734	185.318	219.760	290.292	255.03	255.85	186.14	359.17	325.56	221.41
1871	294.409	281.683	222.455	353.637	288.05	52.86	46.50	235.18	59.33	112.09
1872 B	264.001	18.313	225.158	57.156	321.16	210.31	267.47	110.85	153.15	3.47
1873	233.676	114.678	227.853	120.501	354.18	7.33	127.83	346.85	246.82	254.15
1874	203.350	211.042	230.546	183.846	27.20	164.34	348.19	222.85	340.50	144.84
1875	173.025	307.407	233.241	247.191	60.22	321.36	208.55	98.66	74.17	35.52
1876 B	142.617	44.037	235.944	310.710	93.33	118.80	69.51	334.52	168.09	286.00
1877	112.292	140.402	238.639	14.055	126.35	275.82	249.87	210.53	261.76	177.58
1878	81.967	236.767	241.334	77.400	159.37	72.83	150.23	86.53	355.43	68.27
1879	51.642	333.132	244.029	140.745	192.39	229.85	10.59	322.54	89.10	318.95
1880 B	21.234	69.762	246.732	204.264	225.60	27.99	231.56	104.20	183.03	210.32
1881	350.908	166.124	249.424	267.608	258.52	184.31	91.92	74.21	276.70	101.01
1882	320.583	262.489	252.119	330.953	291.54	341.39	312.28	310.21	10.37	357.69
1883	290.258	358.856	254.815	34.299	324.56	138.31	172.64	186.22	104.04	242.38
1884 B	259.849	95.481	257.514	97.816	357.66	295.78	33.60	61.88	197.97	133.75
1885	229.524	191.848	260.210	161.162	30.69	92.80	253.96	297.68	291.64	24.44
1886	199.198	288.208	262.901	224.505	63.70	249.81	114.32	173.89	25.31	275.12
1887	168.873	24.575	265.597	287.851	96.72	46.83	334.68	49.89	118.98	165.81
1888 B	138.465	121.204	268.289	351.370	129.83	204.27	195.64	285.56	212.90	57.18
1889	108.139	217.567	270.992	54.714	162.85	1.29	56.00	161.56	306.57	307.86
1890	77.814	313.932	273.647	118.059	195.87	158.30	276.36	37.57	40.24	198.55
1891	47.489	50.297	276.382	181.404	228.89	315.32	136.72	273.57	133.91	89.23
1892 B	17.080	146.924	279.082	244.922	262.00	112.76	357.69	149.24	227.84	340.61
1893	346.755	243.289	281.777	308.267	295.02	269.78	218.05	25.24	321.51	231.20
1894	316.430	339.654	284.472	11.612	328.04	66.79	78.41	261.25	55.18	121.98
1895	286.104	76.016	287.164	74.956	1.06	223.81	298.76	137.25	148.85	12.66
1896 B	255.696	172.646	289.867	138.475	34.17	21.95	159.73	12.92	242.78	264.03
1897	225.371	269.013	292.563	201.821	67.19	178.27	20.00	248.92	336.45	154.72
1898	195.045	5.375	295.255	265.165	100.21	335.28	240.45	124.92	70.12	45.40
1899	164.720	101.740	297.950	328.510	133.23	132.30	100.81	0.93	163.79	296.09
1900 B	134.311	198.367	300.650	32.028	166.34	289.74	321.77	236.59	257.72	187.46

TABLE III.—*Continued.*

FOR THE ARGUMENTS.

A. For the different Years. The times are referred to the meridian of Washington.

Years.	XI.	XII.	XIII.	XIV.	XV.	XVI.	XVII.	XVIII.	XIX.	XX.
1850	76.0	326.9	217.8	42.9	24.1	198.4	133.2	172.4	17.5	89.3
1851	63.8	48.3	32.9	112.1	199.4	122.2	214.9	18.1	349.9	106.7
1852 *B*	51.6	130.0	208.5	181.6	14.3	46.6	295.8	223.4	322.1	125.1
1853	39.3	211.5	23.6	250.8	189.7	330.3	17.5	69.1	294.5	142.5
1854	27.1	209.0	198.8	320.1	5.0	254.0	99.2	274.7	266.9	159.9
1855	14.9	14.4	13.9	29.3	180.4	177.8	180.9	120.4	239.2	177.2
1856 *B*	2.7	96.1	189.5	98.8	355.2	109.2	261.8	325.7	211.6	195.6
1857	350.5	177.5	4.6	168.0	170.6	25.9	343.5	171.4	183.9	213.0
1858	338.3	259.0	179.8	237.3	345.9	309.6	65.2	17.0	156.3	230.4
1859	326.1	340.5	354.9	300.5	161.3	233.3	146.8	222.7	128.7	247.7
1860 *B*	313.8	69.2	170.5	16.0	336.1	157.8	227.8	68.0	101.0	266.2
1861	301.6	143.6	345.6	85.2	151.5	81.5	309.5	273.6	73.3	283.5
1862	289.4	225.1	160.8	154.5	326.8	5.2	31.1	119.3	45.7	300.9
1863	277.2	306.5	335.9	223.7	142.2	288.9	112.8	325.0	18.1	318.3
1864 *B*	264.9	28.2	151.5	293.2	317.0	213.4	193.7	170.2	350.3	336.7
1865	252.7	109.7	326.6	2.4	132.4	136.1	275.4	15.9	322.7	354.1
1866	240.5	191.1	141.8	71.7	307.7	60.8	357.1	221.6	205.1	11.5
1867	228.3	272.6	316.9	140.9	123.1	344.5	78.8	67.3	267.5	28.8
1868 *B*	216.1	354.3	132.5	210.3	297.9	269.0	159.7	272.6	239.8	47.2
1869	203.8	75.7	307.6	279.6	113.3	192.7	241.4	118.2	212.1	64.6
1870	191.6	157.2	122.8	348.8	288.6	116.4	323.1	323.9	184.5	82.0
1871	179.4	238.7	297.9	58.1	104.0	40.1	41.8	169.6	156.9	99.4
1872 *B*	167.2	320.3	113.5	127.5	278.8	324.6	125.7	14.8	129.2	117.8
1873	155.0	41.8	298.6	196.8	94.2	248.3	207.4	220.5	101.5	135.1
1874	142.8	123.3	103.8	266.0	269.5	172.0	289.1	66.2	73.9	152.5
1875	130.6	204.7	278.9	335.3	84.9	95.7	10.7	271.9	46.3	169.9
1876 *B*	118.3	286.4	94.5	44.7	259.8	20.2	91.7	117.1	18.5	188.3
1877	106.1	7.9	269.6	114.0	75.1	303.9	173.3	322.8	350.9	205.7
1878	93.9	89.3	84.8	183.2	250.5	227.6	255.0	168.5	323.3	223.1
1879	81.7	170.8	250.9	252.5	65.8	151.3	336.7	14.2	295.7	240.4
1880 *B*	69.4	252.5	75.5	321.9	240.7	75.8	57.6	219.4	268.0	258.9
1881	57.2	333.9	250.6	31.2	56.0	350.5	139.3	65.1	240.3	276.2
1882	45.0	55.4	65.8	100.4	231.4	283.2	221.0	270.8	212.7	293.6
1883	32.8	136.8	240.9	169.7	46.7	206.9	302.7	116.5	185.1	311.0
1884 *B*	20.6	218.5	56.5	230.1	221.6	131.4	23.6	321.7	157.3	329.4
1885	8.3	300.0	231.6	308.3	36.9	55.1	105.3	167.4	129.7	346.8
1886	356.1	21.4	46.8	17.6	212.3	338.8	167.0	13.1	102.1	4.1
1887	343.9	102.9	221.9	86.8	27.6	262.5	268.7	218.8	74.4	21.5
1888 *B*	331.7	184.6	37.5	156.3	202.5	187.0	349.6	64.0	46.8	39.9
1889	319.5	266.1	212.6	225.5	17.8	110.7	71.3	269.7	19.1	57.3
1890	307.3	347.5	27.8	294.8	193.2	34.4	152.9	115.4	351.5	74.7
1891	295.1	69.0	202.9	4.0	8.5	318.1	234.6	321.1	323.9	92.0
1892 *B*	282.8	150.7	18.5	73.5	183.4	242.6	315.6	166.3	296.2	110.4
1893	270.6	232.1	193.6	142.7	358.7	166.3	37.2	12.0	268.5	127.8
1894	258.4	313.6	8.8	212.0	174.1	90.0	118.9	217.7	240.9	145.2
1895	246.2	35.0	183.9	281.2	349.5	13.7	200.6	63.3	213.3	162.6
1896 *B*	233.9	116.7	359.5	350.7	166.3	298.2	281.5	268.6	185.5	180.0
1897	221.7	198.2	174.6	59.9	339.7	221.9	3.2	114.3	157.9	198.4
1898	209.5	279.6	349.8	129.2	155.0	145.6	84.9	320.0	130.3	215.7
1899	197.3	1.1	164.9	198.4	330.4	69.3	166.6	165.7	102.7	233.1
1900 *B*	185.1	82.8	340.5	267.8	145.2	353.8	247.5	10.9	75.0	251.5

TABLE III.—*Continued.*

FOR THE ARGUMENTS.

A. For the different Years. The times are referred to the meridian of Washington.

Years.	XXI.	XXII.	XXIII.	XXIV.	XXV.	XXVI.	XXVII.	XXVIII.	XXIX.	XXX.
1850	179	120	81	11	262	229	70	238	135	185
1851	319	156	352	140	125	171	212	285	119	79
1852 *B*	119	192	261	270	348	113	354	334	105	333
1853	279	227	176	39	212	65	136	22	89	227
1854	78	263	87	169	75	357	279	70	73	121
1855	238	299	359	298	298	299	61	117	58	15
1856 *B*	38	335	271	68	161	241	203	166	43	269
1857	198	10	182	197	24	183	345	214	28	163
1858	358	46	94	327	247	125	127	261	12	58
1859	157	82	6	96	110	67	270	309	356	312
1860 *B*	318	117	277	226	334	9	51	358	342	205
1861	117	153	189	355	197	311	194	46	326	100
1862	277	189	101	125	60	253	336	93	310	354
1863	77	225	12	254	283	195	118	141	205	248
1864 *B*	237	260	284	24	147	137	260	190	280	142
1865	37	296	196	153	10	79	43	238	264	36
1866	196	332	107	282	233	21	165	285	249	290
1867	356	8	19	52	96	323	327	333	233	184
1868 *B*	156	43	291	182	320	265	109	22	218	78
1869	316	79	202	311	183	207	251	70	208	332
1870	116	115	114	80	46	149	31	117	187	236
1871	275	151	26	210	269	91	176	165	171	120
1872 *B*	75	186	297	339	133	33	318	214	157	14
1873	235	222	209	109	356	335	100	261	141	268
1874	35	258	121	234	219	277	242	309	125	162
1875	195	203	32	8	82	219	25	357	110	56
1876 *B*	355	329	304	137	305	161	166	46	95	310
1877	154	5	216	267	169	103	309	93	79	204
1878	315	41	127	36	32	45	91	141	64	98
1879	114	76	39	166	255	347	233	189	48	353
1880 *B*	274	112	310	295	118	289	15	238	33	246
1881	74	148	222	65	341	231	157	285	18	141
1882	233	184	133	194	204	173	300	333	2	35
1883	33	219	46	323	67	115	82	21	346	289
1884 *B*	193	255	317	93	291	57	224	69	332	183
1885	353	291	229	223	154	359	6	117	316	77
1886	153	326	140	352	17	301	149	165	300	331
1887	312	2	52	121	240	243	291	213	245	225
1888 *B*	113	34	324	251	104	185	73	261	270	119
1889	272	74	235	20	327	127	215	309	254	13
1890	72	110	147	150	190	69	357	357	239	267
1891	232	145	59	279	53	11	140	45	223	161
1892 *B*	32	181	330	49	277	313	281	93	208	55
1893	192	217	242	178	140	255	64	141	193	309
1894	351	253	154	308	3	197	206	189	177	203
1895	151	288	65	77	226	139	348	236	162	97
1896 *B*	311	324	337	207	90	81	130	285	147	351
1897	111	0	249	336	313	23	272	333	131	245
1898	270	35	160	106	176	325	55	21	116	139
1899	70	71	72	235	39	267	197	68	100	34
1900 *B*	230	107	344	5	262	209	339	117	85	287

TABLE III.—*Continued.*

FOR THE ARGUMENTS.

B. Variations of the Arguments for the different Months. The times are referred to the meridian of Washington.

Months.	I.	II.	III.	IV.	V.	VI.	VII.	VIII.	IX.	X.
January . .	0.000	0.000	0.000	0.000	0.00	0.00	0.00	0.00	0.00	0.00
February . .	357.425	8.184	0.220	5.378	2.80	13.34	18.71	349.47	7.95	21.29
March . . .	355.098	15.576	0.436	10.236	5.34	25.38	35.62	339.96	15.14	40.52
April . . .	352.523	23.760	0.665	15.614	8.14	38.72	54.33	329.43	23.08	61.81
May	350.031	31.680	0.887	20.819	10.86	51.62	72.44	319.23	30.78	82.42
June	347.456	39.864	1.116	26.197	13.66	64.96	91.16	308.70	38.74	103.71
July	344.964	47.784	1.338	31.402	16.38	77.87	109.27	298.51	46.43	124.31
August . . .	342.389	55.968	1.567	36.780	19.18	91.20	127.99	287.98	54.39	145.60
September .	339.814	64.152	1.796	42.158	21.99	104.54	146.70	277.45	62.34	166.89
October . . .	337.322	72.072	2.018	47.363	24.70	117.44	164.81	267.26	70.04	187.50
November . .	334.747	80.256	2.247	52.741	27.51	130.78	183.53	256.73	78.00	208.79
December .	332.255	88.178	2.467	57.946	30.22	143.69	201.64	246.54	85.69	229.39

Months.	XI.	XII.	XIII.	XIV.	XV.	XVI.	XVII.	XVIII.	XIX.	XX.
January . .	0.0	0.0	0.0	0.0	0.0	0.0	0.0	0.0	0.0	0.0
February . .	359.0	6.9	14.9	5.9	344.3	24.1	336.4	346.9	357.7	32.0
March . . .	358.0	13.2	28.3	11.2	330.1	45.9	315.0	335.0	355.5	61.0
April . . .	357.0	20.1	43.2	17.1	314.5	70.0	291.4	321.9	353.2	93.0
May . . .	356.0	26.8	57.6	22.8	299.3	93.3	268.5	309.3	350.9	124.1
June	354.9	33.7	72.4	28.6	283.6	117.4	244.9	296.1	348.6	156.1
July	353.9	40.4	86.8	34.3	268.4	140.7	222.0	283.5	346.3	187.1
August . . .	352.9	47.3	101.7	40.2	252.7	164.8	198.3	270.4	344.0	219.2
September . .	351.9	54.2	116.6	46.1	237.0	189.9	174.7	257.2	341.6	251.2
October . . .	350.9	60.9	130.9	51.8	221.9	212.2	151.8	244.6	339.4	282.3
November . .	349.8	67.8	145.8	57.7	206.2	236.3	129.2	231.5	337.0	314.3
December . .	348.8	74.5	160.2	63.3	191.0	259.6	105.3	218.8	334.8	345.3

Months.	XXI.	XXII.	XXIII.	XXIV.	XXV.	XXVI.	XXVII.	XXVIII.	XXIX.	XXX.
January . .	0	0	0	0	0	0	0	0	0	0
February . .	14	3	352	11	19	355	341	35	29	351
March . . .	26	6	346	21	36	351	325	66	56	343
April . . .	39	9	338	32	55	346	306	100	85	334
May	53	12	331	42	73	341	288	134	113	325
June	66	15	323	53	92	336	270	169	143	316
July	79	18	316	64	110	331	252	202	171	307
August . . .	93	21	309	75	129	326	233	237	200	298
September . .	106	24	301	86	148	321	215	271	229	289
October . . .	120	27	294	97	166	317	197	305	258	281
November . .	133	30	286	108	185	312	179	339	287	272
December . .	146	33	279	118	204	307	161	373	315	263

In Bissextile Years subtract one day from the date in the first two months.

TABLE III.—*Continued.*

FOR THE ARGUMENTS.

C. Variations of the Arguments in the different Days. The times are referred to the meridian of Washington.

Days.	I.	II.	III.	IV.	V.	VI.	VII.	VIII.	IX.	X.
1	359.917	0.264	0.007	0.173	0.09	0.43	0.60	359.66	0.26	0.69
2	359.834	0.528	0.015	0.347	0.18	0.86	1.21	359.32	0.51	1.37
3	359.751	0.792	0.022	0.520	0.27	1.29	1.81	358.98	0.77	2.06
4	359.667	1.056	0.030	0.694	0.36	1.72	2.41	358.64	1.03	2.75
5	359.584	1.320	0.037	0.867	0.45	2.15	3.02	358.30	1.28	3.43
6	359.501	1.584	0.044	1.041	0.54	2.58	3.62	357.96	1.54	4.12
7	359.418	1.848	0.052	1.214	0.63	3.01	4.23	357.62	1.80	4.81
8	359.335	2.112	0.059	1.388	0.72	3.44	4.83	357.28	2.05	5.49
9	359.252	2.376	0.067	1.561	0.81	3.87	5.43	356.94	2.31	6.18
10	359.169	2.640	0.074	1.735	0.90	4.30	6.04	356.60	2.57	6.87
20	358.338	5.280	0.148	3.470	1.81	8.60	12.07	353.20	5.13	13.74
30	357.508	7.920	0.222	5.205	2.71	12.91	18.11	349.80	7.70	20.60

Days.	XI.	XII.	XIII.	XIV.	XV.	XVI.	XVII.	XVIII.	XIX.	XX.
1	0.0	0.2	0.5	0.2	359.5	0.8	359.2	359.6	359.9	1.0
2	359.9	0.4	1.0	0.4	359.0	1.6	358.5	359.2	359.8	2.1
3	359.9	0.7	1.4	0.6	358.5	2.3	357.7	358.7	359.8	3.1
4	359.9	0.9	1.9	0.8	358.0	3.1	357.0	358.3	359.7	4.1
5	359.8	1.1	2.4	0.9	357.5	3.9	356.2	357.9	359.6	5.2
6	359.8	1.3	2.9	1.1	357.0	4.7	355.4	357.5	359.5	6.2
7	359.8	1.6	3.4	1.3	356.5	5.4	354.7	357.0	359.5	7.2
8	359.7	1.8	3.8	1.5	356.0	6.2	353.9	356.6	359.4	8.3
9	359.7	2.0	4.3	1.7	355.4	7.0	353.1	356.2	359.3	9.3
10	359.7	2.2	4.8	1.9	354.9	7.8	352.4	355.8	359.2	10.3
20	359.3	4.5	9.6	3.8	349.9	15.5	344.8	351.6	358.5	20.7
30	359.0	6.7	14.4	5.7	344.8	23.3	337.1	347.3	357.7	31.0

Days.	XXI.	XXII.	XXIII.	XXIV.	XXV.	XXVI.	XXVII.	XXVIII.	XXIX.	XXX.
1	0	0	0	0	1	0	359	1	1	0
2	1	0	0	1	1	0	359	2	2	359
3	1	0	359	1	2	0	358	3	3	359
4	2	0	359	1	2	359	358	4	4	359
5	2	0	359	2	3	359	357	6	5	359
6	3	1	359	2	4	359	356	7	6	358
7	3	1	358	.2	4	359	356	8	7	358
8	4	1	358	3	5	359	355	9	8	358
9	4	1	358	3	5	359	355	10	8	357
10	4	1	358	3	6	358	354	11	9	357
20	9	2	355	7	12	357	348	22	19	354
30	13	3	353	10	18	355	342	34	29	351

TABLE III.—*Concluded.*

FOR THE ARGUMENTS.

D. Variations of the Arguments in the different Hours.   The times are referred to the meridian of Washington.

Days.	I.	II.	III.	IV.	V.	VI.	VII.	VIII.	IX.	X.
1	359.996	0.011	0.000	0.007	0.00	0.02	0.02	359.99	0.01	0.03
2	359.993	0.022	0.001	0.014	0.01	0.04	0.05	359.97	0.02	0.06
3	359.990	0.033	0.001	0.022	0.01	0.05	0.07	359.96	0.03	0.09
4	359.986	0.044	0.001	0.029	0.02	0.07	0.10	359.94	0.04	0.11
5	359.983	0.055	0.001	0.036	0.02	0.09	0.12	359.93	0.05	0.14
6	359.979	0.066	0.002	0.043	0.02	0.11	0.15	359.92	0.06	0.17
7	359.976	0.077	0.002	0.050	0.03	0.13	0.17	359.91	0.07	0.20
8	359.972	0.088	0.002	0.058	0.03	0.14	0.20	359.89	0.08	0.23
9	359.969	0.099	0.003	0.065	0.03	0.16	0.22	359.88	0.09	0.26
10	359.965	0.110	0.003	0.072	0.04	0.18	0.25	359.86	0.10	0.29
20	359.930	0.220	0.006	0.144	0.08	0.36	0.50	359.72	0.21	0.57

TABLE IV.

PERTURBATIONS OF THE CO-ORDINATES IN UNITS OF THE SIXTH DECIMAL.

Terms multiplied with t. Argument $= M$.

Arg.	ξ'	Diff.	η'	Diff.	ζ	Diff.	Arg.	ξ'	Diff.	η'	Diff.	ζ	Diff.
0	− 10.69	+3.48	−269.53	+0.26	− 25.56	+0.10	45	+ 89.07	+0.26	−176.05	+2.95	− 15.10	+1.26
1	7.21	3.46	269.27	0.38			46	89.33	0.18	173.10	2.94		
2	3.75	3.45	268.89	0.49			47	89.51	+0.09	170.16	2.92		
3	0.30	3.44	268.40	0.59	25.46	0.19	48	89.60	0.00	167.24	2.89	13.84	1.31
4	+ 3.14	3.41	267.81	0.71			49	89.60	−0.07	164.35	2.87		
5	6.55	3.38	267.10	0.81			50	89.53	0.16	161.48	2.85		
6	9.93	3.35	266.29	0.92	25.27	0.28	51	89.37	0.24	158.63	2.82	12.53	1.34
7	13.28	3.32	265.37	1.03			52	89.13	0.32	155.81	2.79		
8	16.60	3.27	264.34	1.13			53	88.81	0.39	153.02	2.75		
9	19.87	3.23	263.21	1.23	24.99	0.38	54	88.42	0.47	150.27	2.72	11.19	1.37
10	+ 23.10	+3.19	−261.98	+1.33			55	+ 87.95	−0.55	−147.55	+2.68		
11	26.29	3.13	260.65	1.42			56	87.40	0.62	144.87	2.64		
12	29.42	3.07	259.23	1.52	24.61	0.46	57	86.78	0.68	142.23	2.60	9.82	1.41
13	32.49	3.02	257.71	1.60			58	86.10	0.76	139.63	2.56		
14	35.51	2.97	256.09	1.71			59	85.34	0.82	137.07	2.51		
15	38.48	2.90	254.38	1.79	24.15	0.55	60	84.52	0.88	134.56	2.46	8.41	1.44
16	41.38	2.83	252.59	1.89			61	83.64	0.94	132.10	2.42		
17	44.21	2.77	250.70	1.97			62	82.70	1.00	129.68	2.36		
18	46.98	2.69	248.73	2.05	23.60	0.64	63	81.70	1.05	127.32	2.31	6.97	1.46
19	49.67	2.62	246.68	2.14			64	80.65	1.11	125.01	2.26		
20	+ 52.59	+2.54	−244.54	+2.20	22.96	0.73	65	+ 79.54	−1.15	−122.75	+2.21		
21	54.83	2.46	242.34	2.27			66	78.39	1.20	120.54	2.15	5.51	1.48
22	57.29	2.38	240.07	2.35			67	77.19	1.25	118.39	2.10		
23	59.67	2.30	237.72	2.40			68	75.94	1.31	116.29	2.04		
24	61.97	2.21	235.32	2.46	22.23	0.81	69	74.63	1.34	114.25	1.98	4.03	1.49
25	64.18	2.12	232.86	2.53			70	73.29	1.38	112.27	1.92		
26	66.30	2.04	230.33	2.58			71	71.91	1.41	110.35	1.86		
27	68.34	1.95	227.75	2.63	21.42	0.88	72	70.50	1.45	108.49	1.80	2.54	1.50
28	70.29	1.86	225.12	2.68			73	69.05	1.48	106.60	1.74		
29	72.15	1.76	222.44	2.72			74	67.57	1.51	104.95	1.68		
30	+ 73.91	+1.67	−219.72	+2.76	20.54	0.98	75	+ 66.06	−1.54	−103.27	+1.62	− 1.04	1.51
31	75.58	1.57	216.96	2.80			76	64.52	1.56	101.65	1.56		
32	77.15	1.48	214.16	2.83			77	62.96	1.58	100.09	1.49		
33	78.63	1.39	211.33	2.87	19.56	1.01	78	61.38	1.60	98.60	1.43	+ 0.47	1.50
34	80.02	1.30	208.46	2.89			79	59.78	1.62	97.17	1.37		
35	81.32	1.20	205.57	2.90			80	58.16	1.64	95.80	1.31		
36	82.52	1.10	202.67	2.92	18.55	1.09	81	56.52	1.66	94.49	1.25	1.97	1.49
37	83.62	1.01	199.75	2.94			82	54.86	1.66	93.24	1.19		
38	84.63	0.92	196.81	2.96			83	53.20	1.67	92.05	1.13		
39	85.55	0.82	193.85	2.96	17.46	1.15	84	51.53	1.67	90.92	1.07	3.46	1.48
40	+ 86.37	+0.73	−190.89	+2.97			85	+ 49.86	−1.68	− 89.85	+1.01		
41	87.10	0.63	187.92	2.98			86	48.18	1.68	88.84	0.95		
42	87.73	0.54	184.94	2.97	16.31	1.21	87	46.49	1.69	87.89	0.89	4.94	1.47
43	88.27	0.45	181.97	2.96			88	44.81	1.68	87.00	0.84		
44	88.72	+0.35	179.01	2.96			89	43.12	1.68	86.16	+0.78		
45	+ 89.07		−176.05		− 15.10		90	+ 41.44		− 85.38		+ 6.41	

3

TABLE IV.—*Continued.*

PERTURBATIONS OF THE CO-ORDINATES IN UNITS OF THE SIXTH DECIMAL.

Terms multiplied with *t*. Argument = *M*.

Arg.	ξ'	Diff.	η'	Diff.	ζ'	Diff.	Arg.	ξ'	Diff.	η'	Diff.	ζ'	Diff.
90	+ 41.44	−1.68	− 85.38	+0.72	+ 6.41	+1.45	135	− 12.15	−0.47	− 91.28	−0.59	+ 24.66	+0.85
91	39.76	1.88	84.66	0.67			136	12.62	0.43	91.86	0.58		
92	38.08	2.67	83.99	0.61			137	13.05	0.40	92.44	0.58		
93	36.41	1.66	83.38	0.56	7.86	1.43	138	13.45	0.37	93.02	0.57	25.51	0.80
94	34.75	1.65	82.82	0.51			139	13.82	0.34	93.50	0.58		
95	33.10	1.63	82.31	0.46			140	14.16	0.31	94.17	0.56		
96	31.47	1.61	81.85	0.41	9.29	1.40	141	14.47	0.28	94.73	0.56	26.31	0.74
97	29.86	1.61	81.44	0.35			142	14.75	0.25	95.29	0.55		
98	28.25	1.59	81.09	0.31			143	15.00	0.23	95.84	0.55		
99	26.66	1.57	80.78	0.26	10.69	1.38	144	15.23	0.20	96.39	0.54	27.05	0.68
100	+ 25.09	−1.55	− 80.52	+0.21	12.07	1.35	145	− 15.43	−0.17	− 96.93	−0.53	27.73	0.63
101	23.54	1.54	80.31	0.17			146	15.60	0.14	97.46	0.52		
102	22.00	1.51	80.14	0.13			147	15.74	0.11	97.98	0.51		
103	20.49	1.48	80.01	0.08	13.42	1.32	148	15.85	0.08	98.49	0.49	28.36	0.56
104	19.01	1.46	79.93	+0.04			149	15.93	0.06	98.98	0.48		
105	17.55	1.44	79.89	0.00			150	15.99	0.04	99.46	0.47		
106	16.11	1.41	79.89	−0.04	14.74	1.29	151	16.03	−0.01	99.93	0.45	28.92	0.51
107	14.70	1.39	79.93	0.08			152	16.04	+0.01	100.38	0.44		
108	13.31	1.36	80.01	0.11			153	16.03	0.03	100.82	0.42		
109	11.95	1.34	80.12	0.15	16.02	1.24	154	16.00	0.05	101.24	0.40	29.43	0.45
110	+ 10.61	−1.31	− 80.27	−0.18			155	− 15.95	+0.07	− 101.64	−0.38		
111	9.30	1.28	80.45	0.21			156	15.88	0.09	102.02	0.36		
112	8.02	1.25	80.66	0.24	17.20	1.20	157	15.79	0.11	102.39	0.34	29.88	0.38
113	6.77	1.22	80.90	0.28			158	15.68	0.12	102.72	0.32		
114	5.55	1.18	81.18	0.30			159	15.56	0.14	103.04	0.30		
115	4.37	1.15	81.48	0.33	18.46	1.15	160	15.42	0.16	103.34	0.29	30.26	0.31
116	3.22	1.11	81.81	0.35			161	15.26	0.16	103.63	0.26		
117	2.11	1.08	82.16	0.37			162	15.10	0.18	103.89	0.24		
118	+ 1.03	1.05	82.53	0.39	19.61	1.10	163	14.92	0.20	104.13	0.22	30.57	0.24
119	− 0.02	1.02	82.92	0.42			164	14.72	0.20	104.35	0.20		
120	− 1.04	−0.98	− 83.34	−0.43			165	− 14.52	+0.22	− 104.55	−0.18		
121	2.02	0.95	83.77	0.45	20.71	1.06	166	14.30	0.23	104.73	0.15	30.81	0.19
122	2.97	0.91	84.22	0.47			167	14.07	0.23	104.88	0.13		
123	3.88	0.88	84.69	0.49			168	13.84	0.24	105.01	0.11	31.00	0.13
124	4.76	0.85	85.18	0.51	21.77	1.02	169	13.60	0.25	105.12	0.08		
125	5.61	0.81	85.69	0.52			170	13.35	0.26	105.20	0.06		
126	6.42	0.77	86.21	0.53			171	13.09	0.26	105.26	0.03	31.13	0.06
127	7.19	0.74	86.74	0.55	22.79	0.97	172	12.83	0.26	105.29	−0.01		
128	7.93	0.70	87.29	0.55			173	12.57	0.26	105.30	+0.01		
129	8.63	0.67	87.84	0.56			174	12.31	0.26	105.29	+0.04	31.19	0.00
130	− 9.30	−0.64	− 88.40	−0.57	23.76	0.90	175	− 12.05	+0.26	− 105.25	+0.06		
131	9.94	0.60	88.97	0.57			176	11.79	0.26	105.19	0.09		
132	10.54	0.57	89.54	0.58			177	11.53	0.26	105.10	0.11	31.19	+0.06
133	11.11	0.54	90.12	0.58			178	11.27	0.25	104.99	0.14		
134	11.65	0.50	90.70	0.58			179	11.02	0.26	104.85	0.16		
135	− 12.15		− 91.28		+ 24.66		180	− 10.76		− 104.69		+ 31.19	

TABLE IV.—*Continued.*

PERTURBATIONS OF THE CO-ORDINATES IN UNITS OF THE SIXTH DECIMAL.

Terms multiplied with t.   Argument $= M$.

Arg.	ξ'	Diff.	η'	Diff.	ζ'	Diff.
180	− 10.76		−104.69		+ 31.19	
		+0.25		+0.19		
181	10.51		104.50			−0.07
		0.24		0.21		
182	10.27		104.29			
		0.24		0.23		
183	10.03		104.06		31.12	
		0.23		0.25		
184	9.80		103.81			0.13
		0.22		0.28		
185	9.58		103.53			
		0.21		0.30		
186	9.37		103.23		30.99	
		0.20		0.32		
187	9.17		102.91			0.20
		0.18		0.35		
188	8.99		102.56			
		0.18		0.37		
189	8.81		102.19		30.79	
		0.16		0.39		
190	− 8.65		−101.80			0.96
		+0.14		+0.40		
191	8.51		101.40			
		0.13		0.43		
192	8.38		100.97		30.53	
		0.11		0.45		
193	8.27		100.52			0.32
		0.09		0.47		
194	8.18		100.05			
		0.07		0.48		
195	8.11		99.57		30.21	
		0.05		0.50		
196	8.06		99.07			0.39
		0.04		0.52		
197	8.02		98.55			
		+0.02		0.54		
198	8.00		98.01		29.82	
		0.00		0.56		
199	8.00		97.45			
		−0.03		0.57		
200	− 8.03		− 96.88			0.45
		−0.05		+0.59		
201	8.08		96.29		29.37	
		0.08		0.60		
202	8.16		95.69			0.52
		0.10		0.62		
203	8.26		95.07			
		0.13		0.63		
204	8.39		94.44		28.85	
		0.15		0.64		
205	8.54		93.80			0.58
		0.18		0.65		
206	8.72		93.15			
		0.21		0.66		
207	8.93		92.49		28.27	
		0.24		0.67		
208	9.17		91.82			
		0.27		0.68		
209	9.44		91.14			0.53
		0.29		0.68		
210	− 9.73		− 90.46		27.64	
		−0.32		+0.69		
211	10.05		89.77			0.69
		0.36		0.70		
212	10.41		89.07			
		0.39		0.70		
213	10.80		88.37		26.95	
		0.42		0.70		
214	11.22		87.67			0.75
		0.45		0.71		
215	11.67		86.96			
		0.48		0.71		
216	12.15		86.25		26.20	
		0.52		0.70		
217	12.67		85.55			0.80
		0.55		0.71		
218	13.22		84.84			
		0.59		0.70		
219	13.81		84.14		25.40	
		0.62		0.70		
220	− 14.43		− 83.44			0.86
		−0.65		+0.69		
221	15.08		82.75			
		0.69		0.69		
222	15.77		82.06		24.54	
		0.72		0.68		
223	16.49		81.38			−0.01
		0.76		0.67		
224	17.25		80.71			
		−0.80		+0.66		
225	− 18.05		− 80.05		+ 23.63	

Arg.	ξ'	Diff.	η'	Diff.	ζ'	Diff.
225	− 18.05		− 80.05		+ 23.63	
		−0.83		+0.65		
226	18.88		79.40			−0.97
		0.86		0.64		
227	19.74		78.76			
		0.90		0.62		
228	20.64		78.14		22.66	
		0.93		0.61		
229	21.57		77.53			1.02
		0.97		0.60		
230	22.54		76.93			
		1.01		0.58		
231	23.55		76.35		21.64	
		1.04		0.56		
232	24.59		75.79			1.07
		1.08		0.54		
233	25.67		75.25			
		1.11		0.52		
234	26.78		74.73		20.57	
		1.15		0.50		
235	− 27.93		− 74.23			1.11
		−1.18		+0.47		
236	29.11		73.76			
		1.21		0.45		
237	30.32		73.31		19.46	
		1.25		0.42		
238	31.57		72.89			1.15
		1.28		0.39		
239	32.85		72.50			
		1.31		0.36		
240	34.16		72.14		18.31	
		1.34		0.33		
241	35.50		71.81			1.20
		1.37		0.30		
242	36.87		71.51			
		1.40		0.26		
243	38.27		71.25		17.11	
		1.43		0.23		
244	39.70		71.02			
		1.46		0.19		
245	− 41.16		− 70.83			1.24
		−1.49		+0.15		
246	42.65		70.68		15.87	
		1.52		0.11		
247	44.17		70.57			1.28
		1.55		0.08		
248	45.72		70.49			
		1.58		+0.03		
249	47.30		70.46		14.59	
		1.60		−0.01		
250	48.90		70.47			1.31
		1.62		0.05		
251	50.52		70.52			
		1.64		0.09		
252	52.16		70.61		13.28	
		1.66		0.14		
253	53.82		70.75			
		1.68		0.18		
254	55.50		70.93			1.34
		1.69		0.24		
255	− 57.19		− 71.17		11.94	
		−1.71		−0.28		
256	58.90		71.45			1.37
		1.73		0.34		
257	60.63		71.79			
		1.75		0.39		
258	62.38		72.18		10.57	
		1.76		0.44		
259	64.14		72.62			1.40
		1.78		0.49		
260	65.92		73.11			
		1.78		0.55		
261	67.70		73.66		9.17	
		1.79		0.60		
262	69.49		74.26			1.43
		1.80		0.66		
263	71.29		74.92			
		1.80		0.71		
264	73.09		75.63		7.74	
		1.80		0.77		
265	− 74.89		− 76.40			1.45
		−1.81		−0.83		
266	76.70		77.23			
		1.81		0.89		
267	78.51		78.12		6.29	
		1.80		0.95		
268	80.31		79.07			−1.46
		1.80		1.02		
269	82.11		80.09			
		−1.79		−1.07		
270	− 83.90		− 81.16		+ 4.83	

TABLE IV.—Continued.

PERTURBATIONS OF THE CO-ORDINATES IN UNITS OF THE SIXTH DECIMAL.

Terms multiplied with t. Argument $= M$.

Arg.	ξ'	Diff.	η'	Diff.	ζ'	Diff.	Arg.	ξ'	Diff.	η'	Diff.	ζ'	Diff.
270	− 83.90	−1.78	− 81.16	−1.13	+ 4.83		315	−123.58	+0.76	−185.72	−3.06	− 16.30	
271	85.68	1.78	82.99	1.20		−1.48	316	122.82	0.86	188.78	3.05		−1.15
272	87.46	1.77	83.49	1.26	3.35		317	121.96	0.95	191.83	3.03		
273	80.23	1.75	84.75	1.32		1.48	318	121.01	1.05	194.86	3.02	17.45	
274	90.98	1.73	86.07	1.38			319	119.96	1.14	197.88	3.00		1.08
275	92.71	1.72	87.45	1.45	1.87		320	118.82	1.24	200.88	2.98		
276	94.43	1.70	88.90	1.51		1.49	321	117.58	1.33	203.86	2.96	18.53	
277	96.13	1.68	90.41	1.56			322	116.25	1.43	206.82	2.93		1.02
278	97.81	1.65	91.97	1.63	+ 0.38		323	114.82	1.52	209.75	2.90		
279	99.46	1.62	93.60	1.69		1.49	324	113.30	1.62	212.65	2.86	19.55	
280	−101.08	−1.60	− 95.20	−1.75			325	−111.64	+1.71	−215.51	−2.83		0.95
281	102.68	1.56	97.04	1.82		−1.11	326	109.97	1.81	218.34	2.78		
282	104.24	1.52	98.86	1.88			327	108.16	1.90	221.12	2.73	20.50	
283	105.76	1.49	100.74	1.94		1.49	328	106.26	1.98	223.85	2.69		0.88
284	107.25	1.46	102.68	1.99			329	104.28	2.07	226.54	2.65		
285	108.71	1.42	104.67	2.05	2.60		330	102.21	2.16	229.19	2.57	21.38	
286	110.13	1.37	106.72	2.12		1.48	331	100.05	2.24	231.76	2.53		0.81
287	111.50	1.32	108.84	2.17			332	97.81	2.33	234.29	2.45		
288	112.82	1.27	111.01	2.23	4.08		333	95.48	2.41	236.74	2.39	22.19	
289	114.09	1.23	113.24	2.28		1.46	334	93.07	2.49	239.13	2.33		0.73
290	−115.32	−1.18	−115.52	−2.34			335	− 90.58	+2.57	−241.46	−2.24		
291	116.50	1.12	117.86	2.39	5.54		336	88.01	2.65	243.70	2.17	22.92	
292	117.62	1.06	120.25	2.44		1.45	337	85.36	2.72	245.87	2.09		0.64
293	118.68	1.01	122.69	2.49			338	82.64	2.79	247.96	2.01		
294	119.69	0.95	125.18	2.54	6.99		339	79.85	2.86	249.97	1.93	23.56	
295	120.64	0.88	127.72	2.59		1.43	340	76.99	2.93	251.90	1.84		0.56
296	121.52	0.81	130.31	2.64			341	74.06	2.98	253.74	1.75		
297	122.33	0.74	132.95	2.68	8.42		342	71.08	3.04	255.49	1.66	24.12	
298	123.07	0.68	135.63	2.73			343	68.04	3.10	257.15	1.56		0.47
299	123.75	0.61	138.36	2.76		1.41	344	64.94	3.16	258.71	1.47		
300	−124.36	−0.53	−141.12	−2.80	9.83		345	− 61.78	+3.20	−260.18	−1.37	24.59	
301	124.89	0.45	143.92	2.84		1.38	346	58.58	3.25	261.55	1.27		0.38
302	125.34	0.37	146.76	2.87			347	55.33	3.29	262.82	1.17		
303	125.71	0.29	149.63	2.90	11.21		348	52.04	3.33	263.99	1.06	24.97	
304	126.00	0.21	152.53	2.93		1.34	349	48.71	3.36	265.05	0.95		0.29
305	126.21	0.13	155.46	2.95			350	45.35	3.39	266.00	0.85		
306	126.34	−0.04	158.41	2.98	12.35		351	41.96	3.41	266.85	0.74	25.26	
307	126.38	+0.03	161.39	3.00		1.30	352	38.55	3.44	267.59	0.64		0.19
308	126.35	0.13	164.39	3.02			353	35.11	3.46	268.23	0.52		
309	126.22	0.21	167.41	3.03	13.85		354	31.65	3.48	268.75	0.41	25.45	
310	−126.01	+0.30	−170.44	−3.05			355	− 28.17	+3.50	−269.16	−0.29		
311	125.71	0.39	173.49	3.05	15.10		356	24.67	3.49	269.45	0.19	25.55	
312	125.32	0.49	176.54	3.05			357	21.18	3.49	269.64	0.08		−0.01
313	124.83	0.58	179.59	3.06		1.20	358	17.69	3.49	269.72	+0.04		
314	124.25	+0.67	182.65	−3.07			359	14.19	3.50	269.68	+0.15		
315	−123.58		−185.72		− 16.30		360	− 10.69		−269.53		− 25.56	

TABLE IV.—*Continued.*

PERTURBATIONS OF THE CO-ORDINATES IN UNITS OF THE SIXTH DECIMAL.

ARGUMENT I.

Arg.	ξ'	Diff.	η'	Diff.	ζ'	Diff.	Arg.	ξ'	Diff.	η	Diff.	ζ'	Diff.
0	−2528	−832	−15741	+187	−22		45	−8406	+706	+13147	+436	+19	
1	3360	826	15554	230		0	46	7700	728	13583	399		+2
2	4180	807	15324	271	22		47	6972	747	13982	360		
3	4987	790	15053	313		+1	48	6225	766	14342	319	21	
4	5777	772	14740	354			49	5459	782	14661	280		1
5	6549	752	14386	393			50	4677	795	14941	238		
6	7301	730	13993	432	21		51	3882	805	15179	195	22	
7	8031	705	13561	469			52	3077	814	15374	154		+1
8	8736	679	13092	504	2		53	2263	820	15528	111		
9	9415	651	12588	539	19		54	1443	825	15639	67	23	
10	−10066	−621	−12049	+572		2	55	−618	+828	+15706	+24		0
11	10687	590	11477	603			56	+210	828	15730	−20	23	
12	11277	557	10874	632	17		57	1038	830	15710	62		−1
13	11834	523	10242	660		3	58	1864	831	15648	106		
14	12357	487	9582	686			59	2695	813	15542	148	22	
15	12844	449	8896	711	14		60	3498	805	15394	191		2
16	13293	411	8185	732	3		61	4303	794	15203	233		
17	13704	372	7453	752			62	5097	780	14970	274	20	
18	14076	331	6701	771	11		63	5877	764	14696	314		
19	14407	290	5930	786			64	6641	746	14382	353		2
20	−14697	−248	−5144	+799	3		65	+7387	+727	+14029	−392	18	
21	14945	206	4345	810	8		66	8114	705	13637	429		2
22	15151	162	3534	820		4	67	8819	681	13208	465		
23	15313	119	2714	827			68	9500	656	12743	500	16	
24	15432	75	1887	832	−4		69	10156	628	12243	534		3
25	15507	−31	1055	834		4	70	10784	599	11709	565		
26	15538	+19	−221	834			71	11383	569	11144	596	13	
27	15525	58	+613	832	0		72	11952	536	10548	625		
28	15467	101	1445	828			73	12488	502	9923	651		4
29	15366	144	2273	820		4	74	12990	468	9272	676		
30	−15222	+187	+3093	+812	+4		75	+13458	+431	+8596	−700	9	
31	15035	230	3905	800		3	76	13889	394	7896	720		4
32	14805	272	4705	786			77	14283	355	7176	740		
33	14533	312	5491	771	7		78	14638	316	6436	758	5	
34	14221	353	6262	753		4	79	14954	275	5678	772		
35	13868	392	7015	734			80	15229	235	4906	786		
36	13476	430	7749	711	11		81	15464	192	4120	796	+1	
37	13046	466	8460	688		3	82	15656	151	3324	805		
38	12580	502	9148	662			83	15807	109	2519	811		4
39	12078	536	9810	634	14		84	15916	80	1708	815	−3	
40	−11542	+569	+10444	+605		3	85	+15982	+23	+893	−817		4
41	10973	599	11049	575			86	16005	−20	+76	817		
42	10374	629	11624	542	17		87	15985	63	−741	814	7	
43	9745	657	12166	508		+2	88	15922	105	1535	809		−4
44	9088	682	12674	473			89	15817	147	2364	803		
45	−8406		+13147	+473	+19		90	+15670	−147	−3167		−11	

TABLE IV.—*Continued.*

PERTURBATIONS OF THE CO-ORDINATES IN UNITS OF THE SIXTH DECIMAL.

ARGUMENT 1.

Arg.	ξ'	Diff.	η'	Diff.	ζ'	Diff.	Arg.	ξ'	Diff.	η'	Diff.	ζ'	Diff.
90	+15670	189	−3167	793	−11	4	135	−12126	406	−8574	673	−24	3
91	15481	230	3960	782			136	12532	369	7901	693		
92	15251	271	4742	768			137	12901	332	7208	710		
93	14980	311	5510	753	−15	4	138	13233	292	6498	727	−21	2
94	14669	349	6263	735			139	13525	254	5771	741		
95	14320	387	6998	715			140	13779	213	5030	753		
96	13933	424	7713	694	−19	3	141	13992	172	4277	762	−19	3
97	13509	459	8407	670			142	14164	132	3515	770		
98	13050	493	9077	645			143	14296	90	2745	775		
99	12557	526	9722	618	−22	3	144	14386	48	1970	779	−16	3
100	+12031	557	−10340	589			145	−14434	7	−1191	780		
101	11474	587	10929	559			146	14441	35	−411	778		
102	10887	615	11488	527	−25	3	147	14406	77	+367	774	−13	2
103	10272	642	12015	494			148	14329	119	1141	769		
104	9630	666	12509	459			149	14210	159	1910	761		
105	8964	689	12968	424	−28	2	150	14051	201	2671	751	−11	3
106	8275	709	13392	387			151	13850	240	3422	739		
107	7566	726	13779	349			152	13610	279	4161	725		
108	6838	745	14128	310	−30	1	153	13331	318	4886	708	−8	1
109	6093	759	14438	270			154	13013	355	5594	690		
110	+5334	772	−14708	230			155	−12658	392	+6284	670		
111	4562	782	14938	190	−31	1	156	12266	427	6954	647	−7	2
112	3780	790	15128	148			157	11839	461	7601	623		
113	2990	796	15276	106			158	11378	493	8224	598		
114	2194	801	15382	65	−32	0	159	10885	525	8822	570	−5	1
115	1393	802	15447	22			160	10360	555	9392	541		
116	+591	801	15469	19			161	9805	584	9933	510		
117	−210	708	15450	62	−32	0	162	9221	610	10443	478	−4	1
118	1008	783	15388	103			163	8611	635	10921	445		
119	1801	786	15285	145			164	7976	658	11366	409		
120	−2587	776	−15140	185	−32	1	165	−7318	679	+11775	374	−3	0
121	3363	765	14955	226			166	6639	698	12149	337		
122	4128	752	14729	265			167	5941	715	12486	298		
123	4880	735	14464	305	−31	1	168	5226	731	12784	260	−3	1
124	5615	717	14159	342			169	4495	744	13044	219		
125	6332	698	13817	379			170	3751	755	13263	180		
126	7030	677	13438	415	−30	2	171	2996	763	13443	139	−4	1
127	7707	653	13023	450			172	2233	770	13582	97		
128	8360	627	12573	483			173	1463	774	13679	56		
129	8987	600	12090	516	−28	2	174	−689	776	13735	14	−5	2
130	−9587	571	−11574	545			175	+67	778	+13749	28		
131	10158	541	11029	574			176	863	774	13721	69		
132	10699	509	10455	602	−26	2	177	1637	770	13652	112	−7	2
133	11208	476	9853	628			178	2407	762	13540	152		
134	11684	442	9225	651			179	3169	753	13388	193		
135	−12126		−8574		−24		180	+3922		+13195		−9	

TABLE IV.—*Continued.*

PERTURBATIONS OF THE CO-ORDINATES IN UNITS OF THE SIXTH DECIMAL.

ARGUMENT I.

Arg.	ξ'	Diff.	η'	Diff.	ζ'	Diff.	Arg.	ξ'	Diff.	η'	Diff.	ζ'	Diff.
180	+3092	+742	+13195	-234	- 0		225	+5845	-751	-14504	-345	- 44	
181	4661	729	12961	274		- 2	226	5094	768	14849	306		+ 2
182	5393	714	12687	313			227	4325	786	15155	267		
183	6107	696	12374	350	11		228	3539	800	15422	225	42	
184	6803	676	12024	388		3	229	2739	813	15647	183		2
185	7479	655	11636	425			230	1926	823	15830	141		
186	8134	632	11211	459	14		231	1103	830	15971	99	40	
187	8766	606	10752	493		3	232	+ 273	836	16070	55		3
188	9372	579	10259	525			233	- 563	839	16125	- 12		
189	9951	550	9734	556	17		234	1402	840	16137		37	
											+ 22		
190	+10501	+529	+ 9178	-586		4	235	- 2242	-839	-16105	+ 76		4
191	11021	499	8592	613			236	3081	835	16099	118		
192	11510	455	7979	639	21		237	3916	830	15981	163	33	
193	11965	420	7340	663		3	238	4746	821	15748	205		5
194	12385	384	6677	686			239	5567	811	15543	248		
195	12769	347	5991	706	24		240	6378	798	15295	290	28	
196	13116	309	5285	724		4	241	7176	783	15005	332		6
197	13425	270	4561	741			242	7959	767	14673	372		
198	13695	230	3820	755	28		243	8726	748	14301	412	22	
199	13925	190	3065	768		3	244	9474	726	13889	450		6
200	+14115	+149	+ 2297	-777			245	-10200	-704	-13439	+488		
201	14263	106	1520	776	31		246	10904	679	12951	524	16	
202	14369	64	+ 734	791		4	247	11583	651	12427	560		7
203	14433	+ 22	- 57	794			248	12234	623	11867	593		
204	14455	- 22	851	796	35		249	12857	592	11274	625	9	
205	14433	64	1647	794		3	250	13449	561	10649	656		7
206	14369	106	2441	791			251	14010	527	9993	684		
207	14263	150	3232	786	38		252	14537	491	9309	712	- 2	
208	14113	191	4018	777		2	253	15028	435	8597	737		7
209	13922	239	4795	768			254	15483	417	7860	780		
210	+13690	-274	- 5563	-738	40		255	-15900	-378	- 7100	+782	+ 5	
211	13416	314	6319	741		2	256	16278	338	6318	801		7
212	13102	353	7060	725			257	16616	297	5517	819		
213	12749	392	7785	706	42		258	16913	254	4698	834	12	
214	12357	430	8491	686		2	259	17167	212	3864	847		8
215	11927	467	9177	663			260	17379	169	3017	858		
216	11460	502	9840	639	44		261	17548	124	2159	866	20	
217	10958	535	10479	612		- 1	262	17672	80	1293	873		7
218	10423	568	11091	584			263	17752	- 35	- 420	876		
219	9854	600	11675	555	45		264	17787	+ 9	+ 456	878	27	
220	+ 9254	-630	-12230	-523	0		265	-17778	+ 55	+ 1334	+878		8
221	8624	657	12753	491		+ 1	266	17723	99	2212	875		
222	7967	684	13244	456	45		267	17624	144	3087	869	35	
223	7283	708	13700	420		+ 1	268	17480	188	3956	862		+ 7
224	6575	-730	14120	-384		- 44	269	17292	+239	4818	+853		
225	+ 5845		-14504		- 44		270	-17060		+ 5671		+ 42	

TABLE IV.—*Continued.*

PERTURBATIONS OF THE CO-ORDINATES IN UNITS OF THE SIXTH DECIMAL.

ARGUMENT I.

Arg.	ξ'	Diff.	η'	Diff.	ζ'	Diff.	Arg.	ξ'	Diff.	η'	Diff.	ζ'	Diff.
270°	−17060	+276	+5071	+840	+42		315°	+14682	+454	+9075	−784	+48	
271	10784	319	6511	826		+6	316	15136	414	9211	785		−6
272	16465	361	7337	809			317	15550	373	8426	805		
273	16104	402	8146	791	48		318	15923	331	7621	805	42	
274	15702	442	8937	770		6	319	16254	288	6799	822		6
275	15260	461	9707	747			320	16542	244	5961	838		
276	14779	481	10454	722	54		321	16786	200	5111	850	36	
277	14260	519	11176	696		5	322	16986	156	4250	861		6
278	13705	555	11872	667			323	17142	110	3380	870		
279	13115	590	12539	636	59		324	17252	65	2505	875	30	
280	−12491	+656	+13175	+805		4	325	+17317	+20	+1626	879		7
281	11835	696	13780	571			326	17337	−25	+745	−881		
282	11149	715	14351	536	63		327	17312	71	−135	880	23	
283	10434	743	14887	499		3	328	17241	116	1011	876		6
284	9692	766	15386	461			329	17125	160	1882	871		
285	8926	749	15847	422	66		330	16965	205	2745	863	17	
286	8137	789	16269	382		3	331	16760	249	3598	853		7
287	7327	810	16651	340			332	16511	291	4438	840		
288	6498	829	16991	298	69		333	16220	333	5263	835	10	
289	5653	845	17289	265		1	334	15887	374	6072	809		6
290	−4794	+872	+17544	+211		1	335	+15513	∓414	−6862	790		
291	3922	841	17755	166	70		336	15099	453	7030	−768	+4	
292	3041	889	17921	166		+1	337	14646	490	8376	746		5
293	2152	894	18043	122			338	14156	526	9007	721		
294	1258	896	18120	77	71		339	13630	561	9790	693	−1	
295	362	897	18151	+31			340	13069	594	10455	665		5
296	+535	895	18137	−14		−1	341	12475	626	11089	634		
297	1430	891	18077	80	70		342	11849	656	11691	602	6	
298	2321	884	17972	105			343	11193	683	12259	568		5
299	3205	875	17823	149		1	344	10510	709	12793	534		
300	+4080	+864	+17628	195	69		345	+9801	−734	−13290	−458	11	
301	4944	850	17380	−239		3	346	9067	756	13748	420		4
302	5794	835	17107	282			347	8311	776	14168	380		
303	6629	817	16783	324	66		348	7535	794	14548	338	15	
304	7446	796	16416	367		3	349	6741	809	14886	332		3
305	8242	775	16008	408			350	5932	820	15183	297		
306	9017	751	15561	447	63		351	5109	834	15437	254	12	
307	9768	724	15075	486		4	352	4275	843	15647	210		2
308	10492	696	14552	523			353	3432	850	15814	167		
309	11188	667	13993	559	59		354	2582	854	15937	123	20	
310	+11855	+635	+13400	593		5	355	+1728	−857	−16016	79		1
311	12490	602	12774	−696			356	871	855	16050	−34		
312	13092	567	12116	658	54		357	+16	854	16039	+11	2	
313	13659	530	11429	687		6	358	−838	849	15984	55		−1
314	14189	493	10715	714			359	1667	841	15884	100		
315	+14682		+9975	−740	+48		360	−2528	−841	−15741	+143	−2	

TABLE IV.—*Continued.*

PERTURBATIONS OF THE CO-ORDINATES IN UNITS OF THE SIXTH DECIMAL.

ARGUMENT II.

Arg.	ξ'	Diff.	η'	Diff.	ζ'	Diff.	Arg.	ξ'	Diff.	η'	Diff.	ζ'	Diff.
0	+ 3698	+255	−14558	+ 58	− 64		45	+12944	+133	− 8037	+220	−287	
1	3953	253	14500	63		−18	46	13077	128	7817	222		−10
2	4206	252	14437	67			47	13205	125	7595	222		
3	4458	251	14370	67	82		48	13330	121	7370	225	297	
4	4709	249	14299	71		17	49	13451	116	7143	227		9
5	4958	248	14223	76			50	13567	113	6914	229		
6	5206	246	14143	80	90		51	13680	108	6683	231	306	
7	5452	244	14058	85		18	52	13788	104	6450	233		9
8	5696	243	13970	88			53	13892	100	6215	235		
9	5939	243	13877	90	117		54	13992	96	5978	237	315	
		241		97							239		
10	+ 6180	+239	−13780	+102		17	55	+14088	+ 91	− 5739	+241		7
11	6419	237	13678	105			56	14179	87	5498	242		
12	6656	235	13573	110	134		57	14266	83	5256	244	322	
13	6891	232	13463	113		16	58	14349	78	5012	245		7
14	7123	231	13350	118			59	14427	74	4767	247		
15	7354	228	13232	121	150		60	14501	70	4520	248	329	
16	7582	226	13111	126		17	61	14571	65	4272	250		5
17	7808	224	12985	130			62	14636	60	4022	251		
18	8032	221	12855	133	167		63	14696	57	3771	252	334	
19	8253	219	12722	137		15	64	14753	52	3519	253		5
20	+ 8472	+216	−12585	+142			65	+14805	+ 47	− 3266	+254		
21	8688	214	12443	145	182		66	14852	43	3012	254	339	
22	8902	211	12298	148		16	67	14895	38	2757	255		4
23	9113	208	12150	153			68	14933	34	2502	255		
24	9321	205	11997	156	198		69	14967	29	2245	257	343	
25	9526	202	11841	159		14	70	14996	25	1988	257		3
26	9728	199	11682	164			71	15021	20	1730	258		
27	9927	197	11518	166	212		72	15041	15	1472	258	346	
28	10124	193	11352	170			73	15056	11	1213	259		
29	10317	190	11182	174		15	74	15067	6	954	259		1
30	+10507	+187	−11008	+177	227		75	+15073	+ 2	− 694	+260	347	
31	10694	183	10831	180		13	76	15075	− 3	434	260		− 1
32	10877	181	10651	183			77	15072	7	174	260		
33	11058	177	10468	186	240		78	15065	12	+ 86	260	348	
34	11235	173	10282	190		13	79	15053	16	346	259		0
35	11408	170	10092	193			80	15037	21	605	259		
36	11578	168	9899	195	253		81	15016	26	865	260	348	
37	11744	163	9704	199		12	82	14990	30	1125	260		+ 1
38	11907	160	9505	202			83	14960	35	1384	259		
39	12067	155	9303	202	265		84	14925	39	1642	258	347	
				204							259		
40	+12222	+152	− 9099	+207		12	85	+14886	− 44	+ 1901	+257		1
41	12374	149	8892	210			86	14842	48	2158	257		
42	12523	144	8682	212	277		87	14794	53	2415	257	346	
43	12667	140	8470	213		−10	88	14741	57	2671	256		+ 3
44	12807	137	8257	215			89	14684	61	2927	256		
45	+12944		− 8037	+218	−287		90	+14623		+ 3181	+254	−343	

TABLE IV.—Continued.

PERTURBATIONS OF THE CO-ORDINATES IN UNITS OF THE SIXTH DECIMAL.

ARGUMENT II.

Arg.	ξ'	Diff.	η'	Diff.	ζ	Diff.	Arg.	ξ'	Diff.	η'	Diff.	ζ	Diff.
90	+14623	− 86	+ 3181	+254	−343		135	+ 7759	−227	+12560	+140	−197	
91	14557		3435	253		+ 4	136	7532		12700	135		+15
92	14486	71	3688	251			137	7303	230	12835	133		
93	14411	75	3939		339		138	7072	231	12966	131	182	
94	14332	79	4189	250		5	139	6838	234	13093	127		16
95	14248	84	4438	249			140	6603	235	13217	124		
96	14160	88	4686	248	334		141	6365	238	13336	119	166	
97	14068	92	4932	246		6	142	6126	239	13452	116		16
98	13971	97	5177	245			143	5884	242	13563	111		
99	13870	101	5421	244	329		144	5641	243	13670	107	150	
		105		241					245		103		
100	+13765	−109	+ 5662	+240		6	145	+ 5396	−246	+13773	+ 99		17
101	13656		5902				146	5150		13872	94		
102	13543	113	6141	239	322		147	4902	248	13966	90	133	
103	13426	117	6377	236		8	148	4652	250	14056	86		17
104	13304	122	6611	234			149	4401	251	14142	82		
105	13178	126	6843	232	314		150	4148	253	14224	77	116	
106	13049	129	7074	231		8	151	3895	253	14301	73		17
107	12915	134	7302	228			152	3640	255	14374	69		
108	12778	137	7529	226	306		153	3383	257	14443	64	99	
109	12637	141	7751	223			154	3126	257	14507	60		
		146		222					258		60		
110	+12491	−149	+ 7973	+219		9	155	+ 2868	−259	+14567	+55		18
111	12342	152	8192	216	297		156	2609		14622	51	81	
112	12190	157	8408	214		10	157	2350	259	14673	46		18
113	12033	160	8622	211			158	2090	261	14719	42		
114	11873	164	8833	209	287		159	1828	261	14761	37	63	
115	11709	167	9042	206		11	160	1566	262	14798	33		18
116	11542	171	9248	203			161	1304	262	14831	29		
117	11371	174	9451	200	276		162	1041	263	14860	24	45	
118	11197	178	9651	197			163	778	263	14884	19		
119	11019	181	9848	195		11	164	515	263	14903	14		18
		181		195					263		14		
120	+10838	−185	+10043	+191	265		165	+ 252	−264	+14917	+ 10	27	
121	10653	187	10234	188		12	166	− 12		14927	6		18
122	10466	191	10422	185			167	275	263	14933	1		
123	10275	194	10607	182	253		168	539	264	14934	+ 1	− 0	
124	10081	197	10789	180		13	169	802	263	14930	− 4		18
125	9884	200	10967	178			170	1065	263	14922	8		
126	9684	203	11142	175	240		171	1328	263	14910	12	+ 9	
127	9481	206	11314	172		14	172	1590	262	14893	17		19
128	9275	208	11486	169			173	1852	262	14871	22		
129	9067	212	11647	164	226		174	2113	261	14844	27	28	
		212		162					261		31		
130	+ 8855	−214	+11809	+158		14	175	− 2374	−260	+14813	− 33		18
131	8641	217	11967	154			176	2634		14778	35		
132	8424	219	12121	152	212		177	2894	260	14739	39	46	
133	8205	222	12271	147		+ 15	178	3152	258	14695	44		+ 18
134	7983	224	12418	144			179	3409	257	14646	49		
135	+ 7759		+12560	+144	−197		180	− 3666	−257	+14592	− 54	+ 64	

TABLE IV.—*Continued.*

PERTURBATIONS OF THE CO-ORDINATES IN UNITS OF THE SIXTH DECIMAL.

ARGUMENT II.

Arg.	ξ'	Diff.	η'	Diff.	ζ'	Diff.	Arg.	ξ'	Diff.	η'	Diff.	ζ'	Diff.
180	− 3666	−255	+14592	− 57	+ 64		225	−12966	−134	+ 8052	−221	+ 257	
181	3921	254	14535	63		+ 18	226	13100	129	7831	224		+ 10
182	4175	253	14472	67	82		227	13229	126	7607	226		
183	4428	252	14405	71			228	13355	122	7381	228	207	
184	4680	250	14334	75		17	229	13477	117	7153	230		9
185	4930	249	14259	80	99		230	13594	114	6923	233		
186	5179	247	14179	84			231	13708	109	6690	234	306	
187	5426	245	14095	89		18	232	13817	105	6456	237		9
188	5671	244	14006	93	117		233	13922	101	6219	238		
189	5915	242	13913	97			234	14023	96	5981	240	315	
190	− 6157	−240	+13816	−101		17	235	−14119	− 92	+ 5741	−242		7
191	6397	238	13715	105	134		236	14211	88	5499	244		
192	6635	236	13610	110			237	14299	84	5255	245	322	
193	6871	234	13500	113		16	238	14383	79	5010	247		7
194	7105	232	13387	116	150		239	14462	75	4763	248		
195	7337	229	13269	122			240	14537	70	4515	249	329	
196	7566	228	13147	126		17	241	14607	65	4266	251		5
197	7794	225	13021	130	167		242	14672	61	4015	252		
198	8019	222	12891	133			243	14733	57	3763	253	334	
199	8241	220	12758	138		15	244	14790	52	3510	255		5
200	− 8461	−218	+12620	−142			245	−14842	− 48	+ 3255	−255		
201	8679	215	12478	145	182		246	14890	43	3000	256	339	
202	8894	212	12333	149		16	247	14933	39	2744	257		4
203	9106	209	12184	153			248	14972	34	2487	258		
204	9315	206	12031	157	198		249	15006	29	2229	258	343	
205	9521	204	11874	160		14	250	15035	25	1971	259		3
206	9725	201	11714	164			251	15060	20	1712	260		
207	9926	198	11550	167	212		252	15080	16	1452	260	346	
208	10124	194	11383	171			253	15096	11	1192	260		1
209	10318	192	11212	174		15	254	15107	6	932	260		
210	−10510	−188	+11038	−178	227		255	−15113	− 2	+ 672	−261	347	
211	10698	185	10860	181		13	256	15115	+ 3	411	261		+ 1
212	10883	182	10679	184			257	15112		+ 150	261		
213	11065	178	10495	187	240		258	15104	8	− 111	261	349	
214	11243	175	10308	191		13	259	15092	12	372	260		0
215	11418	171	10117	193			260	15075	17	632	261		
216	11589	168	9924	197	253		261	15053	22	893	261	348	
217	11757	164	9727	200		12	262	15027	26	1153	260		− 1
218	11921	161	9527	202			263	14997	30	1413	260		
219	12082	157	9325	206	265		264	14962	35	1673	260	347	
220	−12239	−153	+ 9119	−208		12	265	−14922	− 40	− 1931	−259		1
221	12392	149	8911	211			266	14878	41	2190	257		
222	12541	145	8700	214	277		267	14820	49	2447	257	346	
223	12686	142	8486	216		+ 10	268	14776	53	2704	257		− 3
224	12828	138	8270	218			269	14718	58	2960	256		
225	−12966		+ 8052		+ 247		270	−14655	+ 63	− 3216	−256	+ 343	

TABLE IV.—Continued.

PERTURBATIONS OF THE CO-ORDINATES IN UNITS OF THE SIXTH DECIMAL.

ARGUMENT II.

Arg.	ξ'	Diff.	η'	Diff.	ζ'	Diff.	Arg.	ξ'	Diff.	η'	Diff.	ζ'	Diff.
270	−14655	+ 67	− 3216	−254	+ 343		315	− 7737	+229	−12575	−138	+ 197	
271	14588	71	3470	252		− 4	316	7509	230	12713	131		− 15
272	14517	76	3722	252			317	7279	232	12847	130		
273	14441	80	3974	251	339		318	7047	235	12977	126	182	
274	14361	85	4225	249		5	319	6812	236	13103	122		18
275	14276	89	4474	248			320	6576	239	13225	118		
276	14187	93	4722	247	334		321	6337	240	13343	114	166	
277	14094	98	4969	245		6	322	6097	243	13457	110		16
278	13996	101	5214	243			323	5854	244	13567	106		
279	13895	107	5457	242	328		324	5610	246	13673	102	150	
280	−13789	+110	− 5699	−240		6	325	− 5364	+247	−13775	− 97		17
281	13678	114	5939	238			326	5117	249	13872	93		
282	13564	119	6177	237	322		327	4868	250	13965	89	133	
283	13445	123	6414	234		8	328	4618	252	14054	85		17
284	13322	126	6648	232			329	4366	253	14139	80		
285	13196	131	6880	230	314		330	4113	255	14219	76	116	
286	13065	135	7110	228		8 ·	331	3858	255	14295	72		17
287	12930	139	7338	226			332	3603	257	14367	67		
288	12791	142	7564	223	306		333	3346	257	14434	63	99	
289	12649	147	7787	221		9	334	3089	259	14497	59		
290	−12502	+150	− 8008	−219			335	− 2830	+259	−14556	− 54		18
291	12352	154	8227	216	297		336	2571	260	14610	49	81	
292	12198	158	8443	213		10	337	2311	261	14659	45		18
293	12040	162	8656	211			338	2050	261	14704	41		
294	11878	165	8867	208	287		339	1789	262	14745	37	63	
295	11713	169	9075	205		11	340	1527	262	14782	32		18
296	11544	172	9280	202			341	1265	263	14814	27		
297	11372	175	9482	200	276		342	1002	263	14841	22	45	
298	11197	179	9682	196			343	739	263	14863	18		
299	11018	183	9878	194		11	344	476	264	14881	14		18
300	−10835	+185	−10072	−191	265		345	− 212	+263	−14895	− 9	97	
301	10650	189	10263	187		12	346	+ 51	263	14904	− 5		18
302	10461	193	10450	184			347	314	263	14909	0		
303	10268	195	10634	181	253		348	577	263	14909	+ 5	+ 9	
304	10073	198	10815	178		13	349	840	263	14904	9		18
305	9875	202	10993	174			350	1103	263	14895	13		
306	9673	204	11167	171	240		351	1366	262	14882	19	− 9	
307	9469	207	11338	167		14	352	1629	261	14864	23		19
308	9262	210	11505	164			353	1889	261	14841	27		
309	9052	213	11669	160	226		354	2150	260	14814	31	28	
310	− 8839	+215	−11829	−157		14	355	+ 2410	+260	−14783	+ 36		18
311	8624	218	11986	153			356	2670	258	14747	41		
312	8406	221	12139	149	212		357	2929	258	14706	45	46	
313	8185	223	12288	145		− 15	358	3186	257	14661	49		− 18
314	7962	225	12433	142			359	3443	255	14612	54		
315	− 7737		−12575		+ 197		360	+ 3608		−14558		− 64	

TABLE IV.—*Continued.*

PERTURBATIONS OF THE CO-ORDINATES IN UNITS OF THE SIXTH DECIMAL.

ARGUMENT III.

Arg.	ξ'	Diff.	η'	Diff.	ζ'	Diff.	Arg.	ξ'	Diff.	η	Diff.	ζ'	Diff.
0	− 3825	− 61	− 3624	+ 68	+ 18		45	− 5201	+ 5	+ 126	+ 91	+ 2	
1	3886	61	3556	69			46	5196	6	217	90		
2	3947	50	3487	70			47	5190	7	307	90		
3	4006	57	3417	70	+ 5		48	5183	9	398	91	+ 46	
4	4063	57	3347	72			49	5174	11	488	90		
5	4120	55	3275	73			50	5163	12	579	91	1	
6	4175	54	3202	73	20		51	5151	14	669	90		
7	4229	53	3129	75			52	5137	15	759	89		
8	4282	51	3054	75			53	5122	17	848	90	47	
9	4333	50	2979	75			54	5105	18	938	89		
10	− 4383	− 49	− 2902	+ 77	4		55	− 5087	+ 20	+ 1027	+ 88		
11	4432	47	2825	78			56	5067	22	1115	89		
12	4479	46	2747	79	27		57	5045	23	1204	88		
13	4525	44	2668	80			58	5022	24	1292	87		
14	4569	43	2588	80			59	4998	26	1379	87		
15	4612	41	2508	81	4		60	4972	27	1466	87	48	
16	4653	40	2427	82			61	4945	29	1553	87		
17	4693	39	2345	82			62	4916	30	1639	86		
18	4732	37	2263	83	31		63	4886	32	1725	86	+ 1	
19	4769	36	2180	84			64	4854	33	1810	85		
20	− 4805	− 34	− 2096	+ 85	4		65	− 4821	+ 35	+ 1894	+ 84		
21	4839	33	2011	85			66	4786	36	1978	84	49	
22	4872	31	1926	85			67	4750	37	2062	84		
23	4903	30	1841	86			68	4713	39	2144	83		
24	4933	28	1755	86	35		69	4674	40	2226	82		
25	4961	27	1668	87			70	4634	41	2308	82	0	
26	4988	25	1581	87			71	4593	43	2389	81		
27	5013	24	1494	87	3		72	4550	44	2468	79	49	
28	5037	22	1406	88			73	4506	46	2548	80		
29	5059	20	1317	89			74	4460	47	2626	78		
30	− 5079	− 19	− 1229	+ 88	38		75	− 4413	+ 48	+ 2704	+ 78	− 1	
31	5098	18	1140	89			76	4365	49	2780	76		
32	5116	16	1051	90			77	4316	51	2856	76		
33	5132	14	961	90	3		78	4265	52	2932	76	48	
34	5146	13	871	90			79	4213	53	3006	74		
35	5159	11	781	90			80	4160	53	3079	73		
36	5170	10	691	90	41		81	4105	55	3151	72	1	
37	5180	8	600	91			82	4050	55	3223	72		
38	5188	6	510	90			83	3993	57	3293	70		
39	5194	6	419	91	+ 3		84	3935	58	3363	70	47	
40	− 5199	− 4	− 328	+ 90			85	− 3875	+ 60	+ 3431	+ 68		
41	5203	− 2	238	91			86	3815	61	3499	66	− 2	
42	5205	0	147	91	+ 44		87	3754	63	3565	66		
43	5205	+ 1	− 56	91			88	3691	63	3631	66		
44	5204	+ 3	+ 35	91			89	3628	65	3695	64		
45	− 5201		+ 126	+ 91	+ 2		90	− 3563		+ 3758	+ 63	+ 45	

TABLE IV.—*Continued.*

PERTURBATIONS OF THE CO-ORDINATES IN UNITS OF THE SIXTH DECIMAL.

ARGUMENT III.

Arg.	ξ'	Diff.	η'	Diff.	ζ'	Diff.	Arg.	ξ'	Diff.	η'	Diff.	ζ'	Diff.
90	− 3563	+ 66	+ 3758	+ 62	+ 45		135	+ 103	+ 89	+ 5224	− 1		− 4
91	3497	67	3820	61			136	192	90	5223	3		
92	3430	67	3881	60			137	282	90	5220	5		
93	3363	69	3941	58		− 2	138	372	89	5215	6	+ 17	
94	3294	70	3999	58			139	461	89	5209	8		
95	3224	70	4057	56			140	550	90	5201	9		
96	3154	72	4113	55	43		141	640	89	5192	11		5
97	3082	73	4168	53			142	729	89	5181	12		
98	3009	73	4221	53			143	818	89	5169	15		
99	2936	74	4274	51		3	144	907	88	5154	16	12	
100	2862	+ 75	+ 4325	+ 50			145	+ 995	+ 88	+ 5138	− 17		
101	2787	76	4375	49			146	1083	88	5121	18		5
102	2711	77	4424	47	40		147	1171	88	5103	20		5
103	2634	77	4471	46			148	1259	87	5083	22		
104	2557	79	4517	44			149	1346	87	5061	24		
105	2478	79	4561	44		3	150	1433	86	5037	25	7	
106	2399	79	4605	42			151	1519	86	5012	26		
107	2320	81	4647	40			152	1605	86	4986	28		
108	2239	81	4687	39	37		153	1691	85	4958	29		5
109	2158	81	4726	38			154	1776	84	4929	31		
110	− 2077	+ 83	+ 4764	+ 36			155	+ 1860	+ 84	+ 4898	− 32		
111	1994	83	4800	35		3	156	1944	84	4866	34	+ 2	
112	1911	83	4835	33			157	2028	83	4832	35		
113	1828	84	4868	32			158	2111	82	4797	37		
114	1744	85	4900	31	34		159	2193	82	4760	38		5
115	1659	85	4931	29			160	2275	81	4722	40		
116	1574	85	4960	28			161	2356	80	4682	41		
117	1489	86	4988	26		4	162	2436	80	4641	42		
118	1403	87	5014	24			163	2516	79	4599	44		− 3
119	1316	86	5038	23			164	2595	78	4555	45		
120	− 1230	+ 87	+ 5061	+ 22	30		165	+ 2673	+ 78	+ 4510	− 47		6
121	1143	88	5083	20			166	2751	78	4463	48		
122	1055	88	5103	19			167	2827	76	4415	49		
123	967	88	5122	17		4	168	2903	75	4366	51	− 9	
124	879	88	5139	15			169	2978	74	4315	52		9
125	791	89	5154	14			170	3052	73	4263	53		
126	702	89	5168	13	26		171	3125	73	4210	55		5
127	613	89	5181	11			172	3198	71	4155	56		
128	524	89	5192	9			173	3269	71	4099	57		
129	435	90	5201	8		5	174	3340	69	4042	58	− 14	
130	− 345	+ 89	+ 5209	+ 6			175	+ 3409	+ 69	+ 3984	− 60		
131	256	90	5215	5			176	3478	67	3924	61		− 4
132	166	89	5220	3	+ 21		177	3545	67	3863	62		4
133	− 77	90	5223	1			178	3612	65	3801	63		
134	+ 13	90	5224	0			179	3677	64	3738	64		
135	+ 103		+ 5224			− 4	180	+ 3741		+ 3674		− 18	

TABLE IV.—*Continued.*

PERTURBATIONS OF THE CO-ORDINATES IN UNITS OF THE SIXTH DECIMAL.

ARGUMENT III.

Arg.	ξ'	Diff.	η'	Diff.	ζ'	Diff.	Arg.	ξ'	Diff.	η'	Diff.	ζ'	Diff.
180	+3741	+63	+3674	-66	-18		225	+5247	-1	-64	-93		-2
181	3804	62	3608	66			226	5246	3	157	92		
182	3866	61	3542	68			227	5243	5	249	93		
183	3927	61	3474	68	-5		228	5238	7	342	92	-46	
184	3987	60	3405	69			229	5231	8	434	93		
185	4046	59	3335	70			230	5223	9	527	92		
186	4103	57	3264	71	23		231	5214	11	619	92	1	
187	4159	56	3192	72			232	5203	13	711	92		
188	4214	55	3119	73			233	5190	15	803	91		
189	4268	54	3045	74	4		234	5175	16	894	91	47	
		52		75					18		92		
190	+4320	+51	+2970	-75			235	+5159	-18	-986	-91		
191	4371	50	2895	77			236	5141	19	1077	91	1	
192	4421	49	2818	78	27		237	5122	21	1168	90		
193	4470	47	2740	78			238	5101	22	1258	90		
194	4517	46	2662	80			239	5079	24	1348	90		
195	4563	44	2582	80	4		240	5055	26	1438	89	48	
196	4607	43	2502	81			241	5029	27	1527	89		
197	4650	42	2421	81			242	5002	29	1616	88		
198	4692	40	2340	83	31		243	4973	30	1704	88	-1	
199	4732	39	2257	83			244	4943	32	1792	87		
200	+4771	+37	+2174	-84			245	+4911	-34	-1879	-87		
201	4808	36	2090	85	4		246	4877	35	1966	86	49	
202	4844	35	2005	85			247	4842	36	2052	85		
203	4879	33	1920	86			248	4806	38	2137	85		
204	4912	31	1834	86	35		249	4768	39	2222	84	0	
205	4943	30	1748	87			250	4729	41	2306	84		
206	4973	29	1661	88			251	4688	43	2390	83		
207	5002	27	1573	88	3		252	4645	44	2473	82	49	
208	5029	25	1485	88			253	4601	45	2555	81		
209	5054	24	1397	89			254	4556	47	2636	80		
210	+5078	+22	+1309	-90	38		255	+4509	-48	-2716	-80		+1
211	5100	21	1218	90			256	4461	50	2796	78		
212	5121	20	1128	90			257	4411	51	2874	78		
213	5141	17	1038	91	3		258	4360	52	2952	77	48	
214	5158	16	947	91			259	4308	54	3029	76		
215	5174	15	856	91			260	4254	55	3105	75		
216	5189	13	765	91	41		261	4199	56	3180	74	1	
217	5202	11	674	91			262	4143	58	3254	73		
218	5213	10	582	92			263	4085	59	3327	73		
219	5223	8	490	92	3		264	4026	60	3399	72	47	
220	+5231	+6	+398	-92			265	+3966	-61	-3470	-71		
221	5237	5	306	93			266	3905	62	3540	70	+2	
222	5242	4	213	92	-44		267	3842	64	3609	69		
223	5246	1	121	93			268	3778	65	3676	67		
224	5247	0	+28	-92			269	3713	66	3743	67		
225	+5247		-64		-9		270	+3647		-3808	-65	-45	

TABLE IV.—*Continued.*

PERTURBATIONS OF THE CO-ORDINATES IN UNITS OF THE SIXTH DECIMAL.

ARGUMENT III.

Arg.	ξ'	Diff.	η'	Diff.	ζ'	Diff.	Arg.	ξ'	Diff.	η'	Diff.	ζ'	Diff.
270°	+3647	−68	−3808	−64	−45		315°	−149	−93	−5286	+3		+4
271	3579	68	3872	63			316	242	93	5283	5		
272	3511	70	3935	62			317	335	92	5278	7		
273	3441	71	3997	61		+2	318	427	92	5271	8	−17	
274	3370	72	4058	59			319	519	92	5263	10		
275	3298	72	4117	58			320	611	92	5253	12		
276	3226	74	4175	56	43		321	703	92	5241	13		5
277	3152	75	4231	56			322	795	91	5228	14		
278	3077	76	4287	54			323	886	91	5214	17		
279	3001	77	4341	52		3	324	977	91	5197	18	12	
280	+2924	−77	−4393	−52			325	−1008	−90	−5179	+19		
281	2847	79	4445	50			326	1158	90	5160	21		
282	2768	79	4495	48	40		327	1248	89	5139	23		5
283	2689	81	4543	47			328	1337	89	5116	24		
284	2608	81	4590	46			329	1426	89	5092	26		
285	2537	82	4636	44		3	330	1515	88	5066	28	7	
286	2445	89	4680	43			331	1603	86	5038	29		
287	2363	84	4723	41			332	1691	87	5009	30		
288	2279	84	4764	40	37		333	1778	86	4979	32		5
289	2195	85	4804	38			334	1864	86	4947	34		
290	+2110	−85	−4842	−37			335	−1950	−86	−4913	+35		
291	2025	86	4879	35		3	336	2035	85	4878	36		
292	1939	87	4914	34			337	2120	84	4842	38		
293	1852	87	4948	32			338	2204	83	4804	40		
294	1765	88	4980	31	34		339	2287	82	4764	41		5
295	1677	88	5011	29			340	2369	82	4723	42		
296	1589	89	5040	27			341	2451	81	4681	44		
297	1500	89	5067	26			342	2532	80	4637	45	+3	
298	1411	90	5093	24		4	343	2612	79	4592	47		
299	1321	90	5117	23			344	2691	78	4545	48		
300	+1231	−91	−5140	−21	30		345	−2769	−77	−4497	+49		6
301	1140	90	5161	20			346	2846	77	4448	51		
302	1050	92	5181	18			347	2923	76	4397	52		
303	958	91	5199	16			348	2999	74	4345	53	9	
304	867	92	5215	15		4	349	3073	74	4292	55		
305	775	92	5230	13			350	3147	72	4237	56		
306	683	92	5243	11			351	3219	72	4181	57		5
307	591	92	5254	10	26		352	3291	71	4124	58		
308	499	93	5264	8			353	3362	60	4066	60		
309	406	92	5272	6			354	3431	69	4006	61	14	
310	+314	−93	−5278	−5		5	355	−3500	−67	−3945	+62		
311	221	93	5283	3			356	3567	66	3883	63		
312	129	93	5286	3	−21		357	3633	65	3820	64		+4
313	+36	93	5288	2			358	3698	64	3756	06		
314	−57	−92	5288	0			359	3762	63	3690	66		
315	−140		−5286	+2		+4	360	−3825		−3624		+18	

TABLE IV.—Continued.

PERTURBATIONS OF THE CO-ORDINATES IN UNITS OF THE SIXTH DECIMAL.

ARGUMENT IV.

Arg.	ξ'	Diff.	η'	Diff.	ζ'	Diff.	Arg.	ξ'	Diff.	η'	Diff.	ζ'	Diff.
0	+1157	+163	−3275	+71	−1		45	+1474	−146	+2694	+61	+4	
1	1320	150	3204	80			46	1328	148	2755	53		
2	1479	154	3124	87			47	1180	150	2808	45		
3	1633	150	3037	85	−5		48	1030	153	2853	37	−6	
4	1783	141	2942	102			49	877	153	2890	29		
5	1927	139	2840	108			50	724	154	2919	21		
6	2066	132	2732	116	6		51	570	155	2940	13	5	
7	2198	126	2616	122			52	415	155	2953	+4		
8	2324	119	2494	128			53	260	154	2957	−4		
9	2443	113	2366	134	4		54	+106	153	2953	−4	−1	
10	+2556	+105	−2232	+138			55	−47	−153	+2941	−20		
11	2661	98	2094	143			56	200	150	2921	28	6	
12	2759	90	1951	148	10		57	350	148	2893	36		
13	2849	82	1803	151			58	498	146	2857	44		
14	2931	73	1652	156			59	644	143	2813	51		
15	3004	66	1496	158	3		60	787	139	2762	59	+5	
16	3070	57	1338	161			61	926	136	2703	66		
17	3127	49	1177	164			62	1062	132	2637	73		
18	3176	40	1013	168	13		63	1194	127	2564	79	5	
19	3216	31	847	166			64	1321	122	2483	86		
20	+3247	+23	−681	+168	−2		65	−1443	−117	+2399	−92		10
21	3270	14	513	+168			66	1560	112	2307	98		
22	3284	+5	345	162			67	1672	106	2209	103		
23	3289	−4	176	169			68	1778	100	2106	109		4
24	3285	12	−8	168	15		69	1878	94	1997	114		
25	3273	21	+159	167			70	1972	87	1883	118		
26	3252	29	324	165			71	2059	81	1765	122		14
27	3223	38	488	164	0		72	2140	74	1643	127		
28	3185	46	650	162			73	2214	66	1516	129		
29	3139	54	809	159			74	2280	60	1387	132		4
30	+3085	−63	+965	156	15		75	−2340	−52	+1254	−135		
31	3022	70	1118	+153			76	2392	45	1119	137		
32	2952	77	1266	148			77	2437	37	982	139		18
33	2875	84	1411	145			78	2474	29	843	141		
34	2791	91	1551	140	+2		79	2503	22	702	141		
35	2700	98	1686	135			80	2525	14	561	143		+2
36	2602	105	1815	129	13		81	2539	−6	418	142		
37	2497	110	1939	124			82	2545	+2	276	142		
38	2387	116	2057	118			83	2543	9	+134	141		20
39	2271	122	2169	112	3		84	+2534	17	−7	140		
40	+2149	−126	+2274	105			85	−2517	+24	−147	−138		
41	2023	131	2373	+99			86	2493	32	285	137		0
42	1891	135	2464	91	−10		87	2461	30	422	134		
43	1756	139	2548	84			88	2422	46	556	132		
44	1617	143	2625	77			89	2376	53	688	128		
45	+1474	−147	+2694	+89	+4		90	−2323		−816	−128		+20

TABLE IV.—*Continued.*

PERTURBATIONS OF THE CO-ORDINATES IN UNITS OF THE SIXTH DECIMAL.

ARGUMENT IV.

Arg.	ξ'	Diff.	η'	Diff.	ζ'	Diff.	Arg.	ξ'	Diff.	η'	Diff.	ζ'	Diff.
90	− 2323	+ 60	− 816	−125	+ 20		135	+ 2122	+ 21	− 394	+129		− 3
91	2263	66	941	121			136	2143	13	265	131		
92	2197	73	1062	117			137	2156	+ 6	134	131		
93	2124	79	1179	113		− 1	138	2162	− 1	− 3	131		− 7
94	2045	84	1292	107			139	2161	9	+ 129	132		
95	1961	9.	1399	103			140	2152	16	260	131		− 1
96	1870	95	1502	97	19		141	2136	24	391	131		
97	1775	100	1599	91			142	2112	31	521	130		
98	1675	105	1690	85			143	2081	39	650	129		
99	1570	110	1775	79	2		144	2043	45	777	127	8	
100	− 1460	+113	− 1854	− 73			145	+ 1998	− 52	+ 902	+122		
101	1347	117	1927	66			146	1946	59	1024	119	0	
102	1230	120	1993	59	17		147	1887	66	1143	116		
103	1110	123	2052	52			148	1821	72	1259	113		
104	987	125	2104	45			149	1749	78	1372	109	8	
105	862	127	2149	38	4		150	1671	85	1481	104		
106	735	129	2187	31			151	1586	90	1585	99		
107	606	130	2218	23			152	1496	96	1684	95	+ 2	
108	476	131	2241	16	13		153	1400	102	1779	89		
109	345	131	2257	8			154	1298	108	1868	84		
110	− 214	+132	− 2265	− 1			155	+ 1192	−111	− 1952	+ 78		
111	− 82	131	2266	+ 6	4		156	1081	116	2030	72	6	
112	+ 49	130	2260	14			157	965	119	2102	65		
113	179	129	2246	22			158	846	124	2167	59		
114	308	127	2224	28	9		159	722	127	2226	52	3	
115	435	126	2196	36			160	595	129	2278	45		
116	561	123	2160	43			161	466	132	2323	38		
117	684	120	2117	49	5		162	334	135	2361	31	− 3	
118	804	118	2068	57			163	199	137	2392	23		
119	922	114	2011	63			164	+ 62	137	2415	18		
120	+ 1036	+110	− 1948	+ 69	+ 4		165	− 75	−139	+ 2431	+ 8		
121	1146	106	1879	75			166	214	140	2439	0	4	
122	1252	101	1804	82			167	354	140	2439	− 7		
123	1353	97	1722	87	4		168	494	139	2432	15	+ 1	
124	1450	92	1635	92			169	633	139	2417	22		
125	1542	86	1543	98			170	772	138	2395	30		
126	1628	80	1445	102	0		171	910	137	2365	38	5	
127	1708	75	1343	107			172	1047	135	2327	46		
128	1783	68	1236	110			173	1182	132	2281	53		
129	1851	62	1126	115	4		174	1314	130	2228	60	6	
130	+ 1913	+ 56	− 1011	+118			175	− 1444	−127	+ 2168	− 67		
131	1969	49	893	121			176	1571	123	2101	75	+ 4	
132	2018	42	772	124	− 4		177	1694	120	2026	81		
133	2060	35	648	126			178	1814	115	1945	88		
134	2095	+ 27	522	+128			179	1929	−111	1857	− 95		
135	+ 2122		− 394		− 3		180	− 2040		+ 1762		+ 10	

TABLE IV.—Continued.

PERTURBATIONS OF THE CO-ORDINATES IN UNITS OF THE SIXTH DECIMAL.

ARGUMENT IV.

Arg.	ξ'	Diff.	η'	Diff.	ζ'	Diff.	Arg.	ξ'	Diff.	η'	Diff.	ζ'	Diff.
180	− 2040	−106	+ 1762	−101	+ 10		225	+ 68	+172	− 3483	− 8	− 6	
181	2146	101	1661	106			226	260	173	3491	+ 1		
182	2247	95	1555	113			227	433	173	3490	10		
183	2342	89	1442	118	+ 4		228	606	173	3480	18	+ 3	
184	2431	83	1324	122			229	779	172	3462	27		
185	2514	77	1202	126			230	951	171	3435	36	7	
186	2591	70	1074	132			231	1122	170	3399	44		
187	2661	63	942	136	14		232	1292	167	3355	53		
188	2724	57	806	141			233	1459	165	3302	62		
189	2781	48	665	143	3		234	1624	162	3240	70	− 4	
190	− 2889	− 41	+ 522	−146			235	+ 1786	+158	− 3170	+ 78	7	
191	2870	34	376	149			236	1944	155	3092	86		
192	2904	26	227	151	17		237	2099	151	3006	94		
193	2930	17	+ 76	153			238	2250	145	2912	101		
194	2947	10	− 77	154			239	2395	141	2811	109	11	
195	2957	− 2	231	156			240	2536	136	2702	116		
196	2955	+ 7	357	155	+ 2		241	2672	129	2586	123		
197	2952	14	512	156			242	2801	124	2463	130		
198	2938	23	698	155	19		243	2925	117	2333	136	6	
199	2915	32	853	155			244	3042	111	2197	142		
200	− 2883	+ 39	− 1009	−153	0		245	+ 3153	+103	− 2055	+148	17	
201	2844	48	1161	152			246	3256	96	1907	153		
202	2796	55	1313	150			247	3352	88	1754	158		
203	2741	63	1463	147			248	3440	81	1596	162	6	
204	2678	72	1610	144	19		249	3521	72	1434	167		
205	2606	79	1754	141			250	3593	64	1267	170		
206	2527	86	1895	138			251	3657	56	1097	174		
207	2441	94	2033	133	− 2		252	3713	47	923	176	23	
208	2347	100	2166	128			253	3760	38	747	179		
209	2247	108	2294	124			254	3798	29	568	181		
210	− 2139	+114	− 2418	−119	17		255	+ 3827	+ 20	− 387	+183	4	
211	2025	121	2537	113			256	3847	11	204	184		
212	1904	126	2650	107			257	3858	+ 2	− 20	184	27	
213	1778	133	2757	101	3		258	3860	− 7	+ 164	184		
214	1645	137	2858	94			259	3853	17	348	184		
215	1508	143	2952	88			260	3836	26	532	184		
216	1365	148	3040	80	14		261	3810	35	716	182	2	
217	1217	152	3120	73			262	3775	44	898	180		
218	1065	156	3193	66			263	3731	53	1078	179		
219	909	159	3259	58			264	3678	62	1257	178	20	
220	− 750	+163	− 3317	− 50	5		265	+ 3616	− 71	+ 1433	+173		
221	587	166	3367	41			266	3545	79	1606	169	− 1	
222	421	168	3408	34	+ 9		267	3466	88	1775	166		
223	253	169	3442	25			268	3378	96	1941	161		
224	− 84	+172	3467	16			269	3282	−104	2102	157		
225	+ 89		− 3483	− 16	− 6		270	+ 3178		+ 2259	+157	− 30	

36

TABLE IV.—Continued.

PERTURBATIONS OF THE CO-ORDINATES IN UNITS OF THE SIXTH DECIMAL.

ARGUMENT IV.

Arg.	ξ'	Diff.	η'	Diff.	ζ'
270	+ 3178	−112	+ 2259	+152	− 30
271	3066	119	2411	146	
272	2947	106	2557	140	
273	2821	134	2697	134	+ 2
274	2687	140	2831	127	
275	2547	146	2958	120	
276	2401	152	3078	113	29
277	2249	158	3191	106	
278	2091	162	3297	98	
279	1929	168	3395	90	4
280	+ 1761	−172	+ 3485	+ 81	
281	1589	176	3566	74	
282	1413	179	3640	64	24
283	1234	182	3704	56	
284	1052	185	3760	46	
285	867	187	3806	38	5
286	680	189	3844	28	
287	491	190	3872	19	
288	301	191	3891	10	19
289	+ 110	191	3901	+ 1	
290	− 81	−191	+ 3902	− 9	6
291	272	190	3893	19	
292	462	189	3874	27	
293	651	187	3847	37	
294	838	185	3810	46	13
295	1023	183	3764	55	
296	1206	180	3709	64	
297	1386	176	3645	72	6
298	1562	172	3573	81	
299	1734	168	3492	90	
300	− 1902	−164	+ 3402	− 98	7
301	2066	158	3304	105	
302	2224	152	3199	114	
303	2376	147	3085	120	6
304	2523	141	2965	128	
305	2664	134	2837	134	
306	2798	127	2703	141	− 1
307	2925	119	2562	146	
308	3044	112	2416	152	
309	3156	105	2264	158	6
310	− 3261	− 96	+ 2106	−162	
311	3357	89	1944	167	
312	3445	79	1777	171	+ 5
313	3524	71	1606	174	
314	3595	61	1432	178	
315	− 3656		+ 1254	−178	+ 5

Arg.	ξ'	Diff.	η'	Diff.	ζ'
315	− 3656	− 53	+ 1254	−180	+ 5
316	3709	43	1074	182	
317	3752	35	892	184	+ 10
318	3787	25	708	186	
319	3812	15	522	186	
320	3827	− 6	336	187	
321	3833	+ 3	139	186	3
322	3830	13	− 37	186	
323	3817	22	223	186	
324	3795	31	408	185	13
325	− 3764	+ 41	− 592	184	
326	3723	50	773	181	+ 1
327	3673	58	952	179	
328	3615	68	1128	176	
329	3547	76	1301	173	
330	3471	84	1470	169	14
331	3387	91	1635	165	
332	3294	100	1795	160	
333	3194	108	1950	155	− 1
334	3086	115	2106	150	
335	− 2971	+122	− 2244	144	
336	2849	131	2382	138	13
337	2719	135	2514	132	
338	2584	141	2646	124	
339	2443	147	2756	118	2
340	2296	153	2866	110	
341	2143	157	2969	103	
342	1986	161	3064	95	11
343	1825	166	3151	87	
344	1659	169	3228	77	
345	− 1490	+172	− 3298	70	3
346	1318	174	3360	62	
347	1144	177	3412	52	
348	967	179	3455	43	8
349	788	180	3490	35	
350	608	181	3515	25	
351	427	181	3532	17	4
352	246	180	3539	− 7	
353	− 66	181	3537	+ 2	
354	+ 115	179	3527	10	+ 4
355	+ 294	+177	− 3507	20	
356	471	176	3478	29	− 5
357	647	173	3440	38	
358	820	170	3404	46	
359	990	167	3339	55	
360	+ 1157	+167	− 3275	+ 64	− 1

TABLE IV.—*Continued.*

PERTURBATIONS OF THE CO-ORDINATES IN UNITS OF THE SIXTH DECIMAL.

ARGUMENT V.

Arg.	ξ'	Diff.	η'	Diff.	ζ'	Diff.	Arg.	ξ'	Diff.	η	Diff.	ζ	Diff.
0	+ 647	− 32	− 1565	− 10	+ 42		45	− 751	− 25	− 1519	+ 14	− 2	
1	615	33	1575	9			46	770	24	1505	13		
2	582	33	1584	8			47	803	24	1492	15		
3	549	33	1592	8	+ 2		48	827	23	1477	15	+ 45	
4	516	33	1601	8			49	850	24	1462	15		
5	483	33	1608	7			50	874	24	1447	15		
6	449	34	1616	8			51	896	22	1431	16	3	
7	416	33	1623	7	44		52	919	23	1414	17		
8	382	34	1629	6			53	941	22	1397	17		
9	349	33	1635	6			54	962	21	1380	17	42	
		34		6	2				21		18		
10	+ 315	− 34	− 1641	− 5			55	− 983	− 21	− 1362	+ 19		
11	281	33	1646	4			56	1004	20	1343	19		
12	248	34	1650	5	46		57	1024	20	1324	20	3	
13	214	34	1655	5			58	1044	20	1304	20		
14	181	33	1658	3			59	1063	19	1284	20		
15	147	34	1662	4	1		60	1082	19	1263	21	39	
16	114	33	1664	2			61	1101	19	1242	21		
17	81	33	1667	3			62	1119	18	1221	21		
18	47	34	1669	2	47		63	1137	18	1199	22		
19	+ 14	33	1670	1			64	1154	17	1176	23	5	
		33		− 1					17		23		
20	− 19	− 32	− 1671	− 1	1		65	+ 1171	− 17	− 1153	+ 23		
21	51	33	1671	0			66	1188	17	1130	23	34	
22	84	32	1671	0			67	1204	16	1106	24		
23	116	32	1670	+ 1			68	1220	16	1082	24		
24	149	33	1669	1	48		69	1235	15	1057	25	5	
25	181	32	1667	2			70	1250	15	1032	25		
26	212	31	1665	2			71	1265	15	1007	25		
27	244	32	1662	3	+ 1		72	1280	15	981	26	29	
28	275	31	1659	3			73	1294	14	955	26		
29	306	31	1655	4			74	1307	13	928	27		
		30		5					14		27		
30	− 336	− 31	− 1650	+ 4	49		75	− 1321	− 13	− 901	+ 27	6	
31	367	30	1646	6			76	1334	12	874	27		
32	397	29	1640	6			77	1346	13	847	27		
33	426	30	1634	6	− 1		78	1359	12	819	28	23	
34	456	29	1627	7			79	1371	11	791	28		
35	485	28	1620	7			80	1382	11	763	28		
36	513	27	1613	7	48		81	1393	11	735	28	7	
37	542	27	1605	8			82	1404	11	706	29		
38	569	28	1596	9			83	1415	11	677	29		
39	597	27	1586	10			84	1425	10	648	29	16	
		27		10	1				10		29		
40	− 624	− 27	− 1576	+ 10			85	− 1435	− 10	− 619	+ 29		
41	651	26	1566	11			86	1445	10	590	20	− 6	
42	677	26	1555	10	+ 47		87	1454	9	560	30		
43	703	26	1543	12			88	1463	9	531	29		
44	729	25	1531	12			89	1472	9	501	30		
45	− 754		− 1519	+ 12	− 2		90	− 1481		− 471	+ 30	+ 10	

TABLE IV.—*Continued.*

PERTURBATIONS OF THE CO-ORDINATES IN UNITS OF THE SIXTH DECIMAL.

ARGUMENT V.

Arg.	ξ'	Diff.	η'	Diff.	ζ'	Diff.	Arg.	ξ'	Diff.	η'	Diff.	ζ'	Diff.
90°	−1491		−471		+10		135°	−1490		+738		−2	
91	1489	−8	441	+30			136	1480	+10	758	+20		
92	1497	8	411	30			137	1470	10	779	21		
93	1504	7	382	29	−6		138	1459	11	799	20	−24	
94	1511	7	352	30			139	1448	11	818	19		
95	1518	7	322	30			140	1437	11	838	20		
96	1524	6	292	30	+4		141	1425	12	857	19	−1	
97	1531	7	262	30			142	1412	13	875	18		
98	1536	5	232	30			143	1399	13	893	18		
99	1542	6	202	30	6		144	1385	14	911	18	25	
100	−1547	5	−172	30			145	−1371	14	+929	18		
101	1552	5	142	+30			146	1356	15	947	+18		
102	1556	4	113	29	−2		147	1341	15	964	17		
103	1561	5	83	30			148	1326	15	980	16		
104	1564	3	54	29			149	1310	16	997	17		
105	1568	4	−25	29	6		150	1293	17	1013	16		
106	1571	3	+4	29			151	1276	17	1029	16	25	
107	1574	3	33	29			152	1258	18	1045	16		
108	1577	3	62	29	8		153	1240	18	1060	15		
109	1579	2	91	29			154	1222	18	1076	16	0	
110	−1580	1	+119	28			155	−1203	19	+1090	14		
111	1582	−2	147	+28	5		156	1183	+20	1105	+15		
112	1583	1	175	28			157	1163	20	1120	15	25	
113	1583	0	203	28			158	1143	20	1134	14		
114	1584	−1	230	27	13		159	1122	21	1148	14		
115	1583	+1	257	27			160	1101	21	1161	13	0	
116	1583	0	284	27			161	1079	22	1175	14		
117	1582	1	311	27	4		162	1057	22	1188	13		
118	1581	1	337	26			163	1035	22	1201	13	25	
119	1579	2	363	26			164	1012	23	1213	12		
120	−1577	2	+389	26	17		165	−988	24	+1226	13		
121	1574	+3	414	+25			166	965	+23	1238	+12		
122	1571	3	440	26			167	941	24	1251	13	0	
123	1567	4	465	25	3		168	916	25	1262	11		
124	1563	4	489	24			169	892	24	1274	12		
125	1559	4	513	24			170	867	25	1286	12		
126	1554	5	537	24	20		171	841	26	1297	11	0	
127	1549	5	561	24			172	815	26	1308	11		
128	1543	6	584	23			173	790	25	1319	11		
129	1537	6	607	23	·		174	763	27	1329	10	25	
130	−1530	7	+630	23		2	175	−737	26	+1340	11		
131	1523	+7	652	+22			176	710	+27	1350	+10		
132	1515	8	674	22	−22		177	683	27	1360	10		
133	1507	8	696	22			178	656	27	1370	10		
134	1499	8	717	21			179	629	27	1380	10		
135	−1490	+9	+738	+21	−2		180	−601	+28	+1389	+9	−25	

TABLE IV.—*Continued.*

PERTURBATIONS OF THE CO-ORDINATES IN UNITS OF THE SIXTH DECIMAL.

ARGUMENT V.

Arg.	ξ'	Diff.	η'	Diff.	ζ'	Diff.	Arg.	ξ'	Diff.	η'	Diff.	ζ'	Diff.
180	−601	+24	+1389	+10	−25		225	+621	+23	+1509	−8	−2	
181	573	28	1399	9			226	644	23	1501	7		
182	545	28	1408	9			227	667	23	1494	8		
183	517	26	1417	8	−1		228	690	22	1486	9	−39	
184	489	28	1425	9			229	712	22	1477	10		
185	461	29	1434	8			230	734	22	1467	10		
186	432	28	1442	8	26		231	756	22	1457	10	−1	
187	404	29	1450	8			232	778	22	1447	11		
188	375	28	1458	7			233	799	21	1436	12		
189	347	29	1465	7	1		234	820	21	1424	12	40	
190	−318	+29	+1472	+7			235	+841	+20	+1412	−13		
191	289	29	1479	7			236	861	21	1399	13		
192	260	28	1486	7	27		237	882	20	1386	14		
193	232	29	1493	6			238	902	20	1372	15		
194	203	29	1499	6			239	922	19	1357	15		
195	174	28	1505	5	2		240	941	20	1342	16	40	
196	146	29	1510	6			241	961	19	1326	16		
197	117	28	1516	5			242	980	19	1310	17		
198	89	29	1521	4	29		243	999	19	1293	18		
199	60	28	1525	5			244	1018	18	1275	18	+1	
200	−32	+28	+1530	+4	2		245	+1036	+18	+1257	−19		
201	−4	29	1534	3			246	1054	18	1238	19	39	
202	+25	28	1537	4			247	1072	18	1219	19		
203	53	27	1541	3			248	1090	18	1200	21		
204	80	28	1544	3	31		249	1108	17	1179	21	1	
205	108	28	1547	2			250	1125	18	1158	21		
206	136	27	1549	2			251	1143	17	1137	22		
207	163	28	1551	1			252	1160	16	1115	22	38	
208	191	27	1552	1	2		253	1176	17	1093	22		
209	218	26	1553	.			254	1193	16	1071	24		
210	+244	+27	+1554	+1	33		255	+1209	+17	+1047	−24	3	
211	271	27	1554	0			256	1226	15	1023	25		
212	298	26	1554	0			257	1241	16	998	24		
213	324	26	1554	0	2		258	1257	16	974	26	35	
214	350	26	1553	−1			259	1273	15	948	25		
215	376	25	1551	2			260	1288	15	923	26		
216	401	26	1549	2	35		261	1303	15	897	27	4	
217	427	25	1547	2			262	1318	15	870	27		
218	452	25	1544	3			263	1333	15	843	27		
219	477	24	1540	4	2		264	1347	14	816	27	31	
220	+501	+25	+1536	−4			265	+1361	+14	+788	−28		
221	526	24	1532	5			266	1375	14	760	28	+4	
222	550	24	1527	6	−37		267	1389	14	732	29		
223	574	24	1521	6			268	1403	14	703	29		
224	598	+23	1515	−6			269	1416	13	674	29		
225	+621		+1509		−2		270	+1429	+13	+645	−28	−27	

TABLE IV.—*Continued.*

PERTURBATIONS OF THE CO-ORDINATES IN UNITS OF THE SIXTH DECIMAL.

ARGUMENT V.

Arg.	ξ'	Diff.	η'	Diff.	ζ'	Diff.	Arg.	ξ'	Diff.	η'	Diff.	ζ'	Diff.
270	+ 1429	+ 13	+ 646	− 30	− 27		315	+ 1628	− 8	− 726	− 26		+ 5
271	1442	13	615	30			316	1620	9	752	27		
272	1455	13	585	30			317	1611	9	779	26		
273	1467	12	555	30	+ 5		318	1602	9	805	26	+ 18	
274	1479	12	525	30			319	1592	10	831	26		
275	1491	12	494	31			320	1581	11	856	25		
276	1503	12	464	30	22		321	1570	11	881	25		4
277	1514	11	433	31			322	1558	12	906	25		
278	1525	11	402	31			323	1545	13	930	24		
279	1535	10	370	32	6		324	1531	14	954	24	22	
		11		31					14		24		
280	+ 1546	+ 10	+ 339	− 32			325	+ 1517	− 15	− 978	− 23		
281	1556	10	307	32			326	1502	15	1001	23		5
282	1565	9	276	31	16		327	1487	16	1024	23		
283	1575	10	244	32			328	1471	17	1047	23		
284	1584	9	212	32			329	1454	18	1069	22		
285	1592	8	181	31	5		330	1436	18	1091	22	27	
286	1601	9	149	32			331	1418	19	1112	21		
287	1609	8	117	32			332	1399	20	1133	21		
288	1616	7	85	32	11		333	1379	20	1154	21		3
289	1623	7	53	32			334	1359	20	1174	20		
		7		32					21		20		
290	+ 1630	+ 6	+ 21	− 31	6		335	+ 1338	− 21	− 1194	− 20		
291	1636	6	− 10	32			336	1317	22	1214	20		30
292	1642	6	42	31			337	1295	23	1233	19		
293	1647	5	73	32			338	1272	23	1252	19		
294	1652	5	105	32	− 5		339	1249	24	1270	18		4
295	1657	5	137	32			340	1225	24	1288	18		
296	1661	4	168	31			341	1201	24	1306	18		
297	1664	3	199	31			342	1176	25	1323	17		34
298	1667	3	230	31	6		343	1150	26	1340	17		
299	1669	2	261	31			344	1124	26	1356	16		
		2		31					27		16		
300	+ 1671	+ 1	− 292		+ 1		345	+ 1097	− 27	+ 1372	− 16		3
301	1672	+ 1	322	− 30			346	1070	27	1388	16		
302	1673	0	353	31			347	1042	28	1403	15		
303	1673	0	383	30			348	1014	28	1418	15	37	
304	1673	− 1	413	30	6		349	986	28	1433	15		
305	1672	2	443	30			350	957	29	1447	14		
306	1670	2	472	29			351	927	30	1460	13		3
307	1668	2	501	29	7		352	897	30	1474	14		
308	1665	3	530	29			353	867	30	1487	13		
309	1662	3	559	29	6		354	837	30	1499	12	40	
		4		29					31		12		
310	+ 1658	− 5	− 588	− 28			355	+ 806	− 31	− 1511	− 12		
311	1653	5	616	28			356	775	31	1523	12		+ 2
312	1648	5	644	28	+ 13		357	743	32	1534	11		
313	1642	6	671	27			358	711	32	1545	11		
314	1635	7	699	28			359	679	32	1555	10		
315	+ 1628	− 7	− 726	− 27	+ 5		360	+ 647	− 32	− 1565	− 10		+ 42

TABLE IV.—Continued.

PERTURBATIONS OF THE CO-ORDINATES IN UNITS OF THE SIXTH DECIMAL.

ARGUMENT VI.

Arg.	ξ'	Diff.	η'	Diff.	ζ'	Diff.	Arg.	ξ'	Diff.	η'	Diff.	ζ'	Diff.
0	− 308	− 23	+ 364	− 30	+ 9		180	+ 248	+ 50	− 511	+ 22	− 9	
5	331	21	334	29			185	298	48	480	26		
10	352	18	305	30	8		190	346	46	463	31	8	
15	370	16	275	30			195	392	43	431	30		
20	380	14	245	30	6		200	435	39	395	41	6	
25	400	13	214	31			205	474	35	354	46		
30	412	10	184	30	5		210	509	31	308	40	5	
35	422	9	153	31			215	540	25	259	53		
40	431	7	122	31	3		220	565	20	206	56	3	
45	438	5	91	31			225	585	14	151	58		
50	− 443	− 4	+ 60	− 32	+ 1		230	+ 599	+ 7	− 93	+ 60	− 1	
55	447	2	+ 28	33			235	606	+ 1	− 33	59		
60	449	− 1	− 5	33	− 1		240	607	− 6	+ 26	60	+ 1	
65	450	+ 1	38	33			245	601	12	86	59		
70	449	4	71	34	3		250	589	19	145	59	3	
75	445	6	105	34			255	570	24	202	57		
80	439	8	139	34	5		260	546	31	257	55	5	
85	431	11	174	35			265	515	36	308	51		
90	420	14	208	34	6		270	479	40	355	47	6	
95	406	17	243	35			275	439	44	398	43		
100	− 390	+ 20	− 279	− 33	− 8		280	+ 395	− 48	+ 436	+ 38	+ 8	
105	369	23	311	33			285	347	50	468	32		
110	346	26	344	32	9		290	297	51	495	27	9	
115	320	29	376	30			295	246	53	515	20		
120	291	33	406	28	10		300	193	53	530	15	10	
125	258	36	434	25			305	140	53	539	9		
130	222	39	459	23	11		310	88	52	543	+ 4	11	
135	184	42	482	20			315	+ 36	52	541	− 2		
140	142	44	502	16	11		320	− 13	49	535	6	11	
145	98	46	518	13			325	60	47	524	11		
150	− 52	+ 48	− 531	− 8	− 11		330	− 105	− 42	+ 509	− 19	+ 11	
155	− 4	49	539	− 4			335	141	38	490	21		
160	+ 45	50	543	+ 1	11		340	185	35	469	24	11	
165	95	52	542	5			345	220	33	445	26		
170	147	51	537	11	10		350	253	29	419	26	10	
175	198	+ 50	526	+ 15			355	282	− 26	292	27		
180	+ 248		− 511		− 9		360	− 308		+ 364	− 28	+ 9	

TABLE IV.—*Continued.*

PERTURBATIONS OF THE CO-ORDINATES IN UNITS OF THE SIXTH DECIMAL.

ARGUMENT VII.

Arg.	ξ'	Diff.	η'	Diff.	ζ'	Diff.	Arg.	ξ'	Diff.	η'	Diff.	ζ'	Diff.
0	− 196	+ 41	− 464	− 16	+ 3		180	+ 194	− 41	+ 464	+ 15	− 3	
5	155	43	480	11			185	153	43	479	12		
10	112	43	491	8	3		190	110	43	491	7	3	
15	69	44	499	− 5			195	67	43	498	+ 4		
20	− 25	44	504	0	3		200	+ 23	44	502	0	3	
25	+ 20	45	504	+ 4			205	− 21	44	502	− 3		
30	64	44	500	7	3		210	65	44	499		3	
35	107	43	493	11			215	108	43	491	8		
40	150	43	482	15	2		220	150	42	480	11	2	
45	192	42	467	19			225	192	42	465	15		
		40		19					40		18		
50	+ 232	+ 38	− 448	+ 22	+ 2		230	− 232	− 38	+ 447	− 22	− 2	
55	270	37	426	23			235	270	36	425	25		
60	307	-34	401	26	2		240	306	34	400	28	2	
65	341	31	373	31			245	340	34	372	31		
70	372	29	342	33	2		250	371	31	341	33	2	
75	401	26	309	36			255	399	28	308	36		
80	427	22	273	39	1		260	425	26	272	38	1	
85	449	19	234	40			265	447	22	234	38		
90	468	15	194	40	+ 1		270	466	19	194	40	− 1	
95	483		153	41			275	481	15	153	41		
		11		43					11		42		
100	+ 494	+ 8	− 110	+ 43	0		280	− 492	− 8	+ 111	− 43	0	
105	502	+ 4	67	44			285	500	− 5	68	44		
110	506	0	− 23	44	0		290	505	0	+ 24	44	0	
115	506	− 4	+ 21	44			295	505	+ 4	− 19	44		
120	502	7	65	43	− 1		300	501	7	63	43	+ 1	
125	495	12	108	42			305	494	11	106	43		
130	483	15	150	42	1		310	483	15	149	41	1	
135	468	19	192	40			315	468	18	190	40		
140	449	22	232	38	1		320	450	22	230	40	1	
145	427		270	36			325	428		268	38		
		25		36					25		36		
150	+ 402	− 28	+ 306	+ 34	− 2		330	− 403	+ 28	− 304	− 34	+ 2	
155	374	32	340	01			335	375	31	338	31		
160	342	34	371	28	2		340	344	31	369	29	2	
165	308	36	399	25			345	310	36	398	25		
170	272	38	424	20	2		350	274	36	423	23	2	
175	234	− 40	446	+ 18			355	236	+ 40	446	− 18		
180	+ 194		+ 464		− 3		360	− 196		− 464		+ 3	

43

TABLE IV.—*Continued.*

PERTURBATIONS OF THE CO-ORDINATES IN UNITS OF THE SIXTH DECIMAL.

ARGUMENT VIII.

Arg.	ξ'	Diff.	η'	Diff.	ζ'	Diff.	Arg.	ξ'	Diff.	η'	Diff.	ζ'	Diff.
0	+ 24	+ 6	+ 122	– 2	+ 8		180	– 17	– 10	– 143	0	– 8	
5	30	7	120	1			185	27	10	143	+ 1	8	
10	37	7	119	0	8		190	37	11	142	1		
15	44	7	119	1			195	48	12	141	2		
20	52	8	118	1	7		200	60	13	139	3	7	
25	61	9	117	1			205	73	13	136	4		
30	70	0	115	2	6		210	86	13	132	6	6	
35	81	11	112	3			215	99	13	126	7		
40	92	11	108	4	6		220	112	13	119	9	6	
45	104	12	103	5			225	125	13	110	11		
		11		7					13		11		
50	+ 115	+ 12	+ 96	– 10	+ 5		230	– 138	– 11	– 99	+ 13	– 5	
55	127	12	86	11			235	149	11	86	15		
60	138	11	75	12	3		240	160	8	71	17	3	
65	147	9	63	14			245	168	7	54	17		
70	155	8	49	16	2		250	175	4	37	19	2	
75	162	7	33	17			255	179	– 1	– 18	19		
80	166	4	+ 16	17	+ 1		260	180	+ 2	+ 1	19	– 1	
85	168	+ 2	– 1	17			265	178	3	21	20		
90	168	0	19	18	1		270	175	7	40	19	+ 1	
95	165	– 3	36	17			275	168	8	59	10		
		5		17							17		
100	+ 160	– 7	– 53	– 16	– 2		280	– 160	+ 11	+ 76	+ 15	+ 2	
105	153	9	69	15			285	149	13	91	14		
110	144	10	84	13	3		290	136	14	105	11	3	
115	134	11	97	11			295	122	15	116	0		
120	123	13	108	0	5		300	107	15	125	6	5	
125	110	13	117	8			305	92	15	131	5		
130	97	13	125	7	6		310	77	14	136	2	6	
135	84	13	132	4			315	63	14	138	+ 1		
140	71	12	136	3	6		320	49	14	139	– 1	6	
145	59	12	139	3			325	36	13	138	1		
		12		3					12		1		
150	+ 47	– 12	– 142	– 1	7		330	– 24	+ 10	+ 137	– 3	+ 7	
155	35	11	143	0			335	14	9	134	3		
160	24	10	143	– 1	8		340	– 5	8	131	3	8	
165	14	11	144	0			345	+ 3	8	128	2		
170	+ 3	10	144	+ 1	8		350	11	6	126	2	8	
175	– 7	– 10	143	0			355	17	+ 7	124	2		
180	– 17		– 143		– 8		360	+ 24		+ 122	– 2	+ 8	

TABLE IV.—*Continued.*

PERTURBATIONS OF THE CO-ORDINATES IN UNITS OF THE SIXTH DECIMAL.

ARGUMENT IX.

Arg.	ξ'	Diff.	η'	Diff	ζ'	Diff.	Arg.	ξ'	Diff.	η'	Diff.	ζ'	Diff.
°							°						
0	+ 183	+ 3	+ 18	+ 16	+ 1		180	− 157	− 1	+ 18	− 11	+ 1	
5	180	4	34	16			185	158	0	+ 7	12		
10	176	6	50	16	3		190	158	+ 1	− 5	11	0	
15	170	7	66	15			195	157	2	16	12		
20	163	9	81	14	5		200	155	3	28	11	− 1	
25	154	10	95	12			205	152	4	39	12		
30	144	11	107	12	7		210	148	5	51	11	2	
35	133	12	119	10			215	143	6	62	11		
40	121	13	129	9	8		220	137	7	73	11	3	
45	108	13	138	8			225	130	8	84	11		
50	+ 95	− 14	+ 146	+ 7	+ 9		230	− 122	+ 9	− 95	− 11	− 4	
55	81	15	153	5			235	113	10	106	10		
60	66	14	158	4	10		240	103	12	116	9	6	
65	52	15	162	3			245	91	12	125	8		
70	37	15	165	+ 1	11		250	79	13	133	8	7	
75	22	14	166	0			255	66	15	141	6		
80	+ 8	14	166	− 1	11		260	51	15	147	6	7	
85	− 6	14	165	2			265	36	16	152	5		
90	20	13	163	3	10		270	20	16	156	4	8	
95	33	13	160	4			275	− 4	16	158	2		
100	− 46	− 12	+ 156	− 4	+ 10		280	+ 12	+ 17	− 159	− 1	− 8	
105	58	12	152	6			285	29	17	159	0		
110	70	11	146	6	9		290	46	17	156	+ 3	8	
115	81	10	140	7			295	63	17	152	4		
120	91	10	133	8	8		300	80	16	147	5	8	
125	101	9	125	8			305	96	15	139	8		
130	110	8	117	8	7		310	111	14	130	9	7	
135	118	8	109	8			315	125	12	120	10		
140	125	7	100	9	5		320	137	12	109	12	6	
145	132	7	90	10			325	149	10	95	13		
150	− 138	− 5	+ 81	− 10	+ 4		330	+ 159	+ 8	− 81	+ 10	− 5	
155	143	4	71	10			335	167	7	65	16		
160	147	4	61	11	3		340	174	5	49	16	3	
165	151	3	50	10			345	179	3	33	17		
170	154	2	40	11	2		350	182	+ 1	− 16	17	− 1	
175	156	− 1	29	11			355	183	0	+ 1	17		
180	− 157		+ 18	−11	+ 1		360	+ 183	0	+ 18	+ 17	+ 1	

TABLE IV.—*Continued.*

PERTURBATIONS OF THE CO-ORDINATES IN UNITS OF THE SIXTH DECIMAL.

ARGUMENT X.

Arg.	ξ'	Diff.	η'	Diff.	Arg.	ξ'	Diff.	η'	Diff.
0	-38	-5	+60	-3	180	+37	+5	-63	+4
5	43	4	57	4	185	42	5	59	4
10	47	5	53	4	190	47	5	55	4
15	52	4	49	5	195	52	5	51	4
20	56	3	44	5	200	56	4	46	5
25	59	3	39	5	205	60	4	41	5
30	62	3	34	6	210	64	4	36	6
35	65	3	29	5	215	67	3	30	6
40	67	2	23	6	220	69	2	21	6
45	69	2	17	6	225	71	2	18	6
		1		6			1		7
50	-70	-1	+11	-6	230	+72	+1	-11	+6
55	71	0	+5	6	235	73	0	-5	6
60	71	+1	-1	6	240	73	0	+1	7
65	70	1	7	6	245	73	-1	8	6
70	69	1	13	6	250	72	2	14	6
75	68	2	19	6	255	70	2	20	6
80	66	2	25	5	260	68	3	26	6
85	64	2	30	6	265	65	3	32	6
90	61	3	36	5	270	62	3	38	6
95	58	3	41	5	275	59	4	43	5
		4		5			5		4
100	-54	+4	-46	-4	280	+55	-5	+48	+5
105	50	4	50	5	285	50	5	53	4
110	46	5	55	4	290	45	5	57	4
115	41	5	59	3	295	40	6	61	3
120	36	5	62	4	300	34	6	64	2
125	30	6	65	3	305	28	6	66	2
130	25	5	67	2	310	22	6	68	2
135	19	6	69	2	315	16	6	70	1
140	13	6	71	2	320	10	6	71	1
145	-6	7	72	-1	325	+4	6	72	+1
		6		0			7		0
150	0	+6	+72	0	330	-2	-7	+72	-1
155	+6	6	72	0	335	9	6	71	1
160	13	7	71	+1	340	15	6	70	2
165	19	6	70	1	345	21	6	68	2
170	25	6	68	2	350	27	5	66	2
175	31	6	65	3	355	32	-6	63	3
180	+37	+6	-63	+2	360	-38		+60	-3

ARGUMENT XI.

Arg.	ξ'	Diff.	η'	Diff.	Arg.	ξ'	Diff.	η'	Diff.
0	-27	+14	-94	+1	180	+27	+3	+2	-2
5	-13	14	95	-1	185	30	3	0	2
10	+1	14	94	4	190	32	2	-3	3
15	14	13	90	6	195	34	2	6	3
20	26	12	84	6	200	36	2	10	4
25	36	10	77	7	205	38	2	15	5
30	44	8	68	9	210	40	2	20	5
35	50	6	58	10	215	41	+1	25	5
40	54	6	48	10	220	41	0	31	6
45	55	+1	37	11	225	41	0	37	6
		0		10			-1		7
50	+55	-2	+27	-9	230	+40	-3	-44	-7
55	53	3	18	8	235	37	3	51	8
60	50	5	10	8	240	34	5	59	7
65	45	5	+4	6	245	29	5	66	7
70	40	5	-2	6	250	22	7	72	6
75	34	6	6	4	255	14	8	78	4
80	28	6	8	2	260	+5	10	82	3
85	22	6	9	1	265	-5	11	85	-2
90	16	6	10	-1	270	16	12	87	+1
95	12	4	9	+1	275	22	13	86	2
		4		2			13		2
100	+8	-3	-7	+2	280	-41	-12	-84	+5
105	5	3	5	2	285	53	12	79	7
110	3	-2	-2	3	290	65	11	72	9
115	1	-2	+1	2	295	76	9	63	12
120	1	0	3	2	300	85	7	51	13
125	1	+1	5	2	305	92	6	38	13
130	3	1	7	2	310	98	6	24	14
135	5	2	9	2	315	101	3	-9	15
140	7	2	10	+1	320	102	-1	+7	16
145	9	2	10	0	325	100	+2	23	16
		3		0			5		15
150	+12	+2	+10	0	330	-95	+7	+38	+14
155	14	2	10	0	335	88	7	52	13
160	17	3	9	-1	340	79	9	65	11
165	20	3	8	1	345	68	11	76	9
170	22	2	6	2	350	55	13	85	6
175	25	3	4	2	355	41	14	91	6
180	+27	+2	+2	-2	360	-27	+14	+94	+3

TABLE IV.—*Continued.*

PERTURBATIONS OF THE CO-ORDINATES IN UNITS OF THE SIXTH DECIMAL.

	ARGUMENT XII.					ARGUMENT XIII.					ARGUMENT XIV.			
Arg.	ξ'	Diff.	η'	Diff.	Arg.	ξ'	Diff.	η'	Diff.	Arg.	ξ'	Diff.	η'	Diff.
°					°					°				
0	+ 3		+ 12		0	+ 13		+ 12		0	+ 3		+ 23	
		− 7		− 1			− 3		+ 2			+ 4		0
10	− 4		11		10	10		14		10	7		23	
		5		4			2		1			3		0
20	9		7		20	8		15		20	10		23	
		3		6			3		1			4		− 1
30	12		+ 1		30	5		16		30	14		22	
		− 1		6			3		1			3		2
40	13		− 5		40	+ 2		17		40	17		20	
		+ 2		6			3		0			2		3
50	11		11		50	− 1		17		50	19		17	
		4		4			3		− 1			2		3
60	7		15		60	4		16		60	21		14	
		6		− 3			3		1			+ 2		3
70	− 1		18		70	7		15		70	23		10	
		6		0			2		2			0		4
80	+ 5		18		80	9		13		80	23		6	
		6		+ 2			2		1			0		4
90	11		16		90	11		12		90	23		+ 2	
		6		+ 4			2		2			− 1		4
100	+ 17		− 12		100	− 13		+ 10		100	+ 22		− 3	
		+ 4		5			− 1		− 3			− 2		5
110	21		− 7		110	14		7		110	20		7	
		+ 1		7			1		2			2		− 4
120	22		0		120	15		5		120	18		11	
		0		7			− 1		3			3		4
130	22		+ 7		130	16		+ 2		130	15		14	
		− 2		7			0		2			4		3
140	20		14		140	16		0		140	11		17	
		4		6			· 0		3			4		3
150	16		20		150	16		3		150	7		20	
		6		4			+ 1		2			4		2
160	10		24		160	15		5		160	+ 3		22	
		6		3			1		3			4		− 1
170	+ 4		27		170	14		8		170	− 1		23	
		7		+ 1			1		2			4		0
180	− 3		28		180	13		10		180	5		23	
		7		− 1			2		2			4		0
190	10		27		190	11		12		190	9		23	
		7		3			2		2			4		+ 1
200	− 17		+ 24		200	− 9		14		200	− 13		− 22	
		− 5		− 6			+ 3		2			− 3		+ 2
210	22		18		210	6		15		210	16		20	
		4		6			2		− 1			2		2
220	26		12		220	4		16		220	18		18	
		− 2		8			3		− 1			2		3
230	28		+ 4		230	− 1		17		230	20		15	
		0		8			3		0			1		3
240	26		− 5		240	+ 2		17		240	21		12	
		+ 3		8			3		0			− 1		3
250	25		13		250	5		17		250	22		9	
		6		6			3		+ 1			0		4
260	19		19		260	8		16		260	22		5	
		7		4			3		2			+ 1		3
270	12		23		270	11		14		270	21		− 2	
		9		− 2			3		2			1		4
280	− 3		25		280	13		12		280	20		+ 2	
		8		+ 1			2		3			2		4
290	+ 5		24		290	15		9		290	18		6	
		7		4			2		3			2		3
300	+ 12		− 20		300	+ 17		− 6		300	− 16		+ 9	
		+ 5		+ 6			+ 1		+ 3			+ 3		+ 4
310	17		14		310	18		− 3		310	13		13	
		+ 2		7			0		3			3		3
320	19		− 7		320	18		0		320	10		16	
		− 1		7			0		4			3		3
330	18		0		330	18		+ 4		330	7		19	
		3		6			− 1		3			3		2
340	15		+ 6		340	17		7		340	− 4		21	
		5		4			2		3			4		1
350	10		10		350	15		10		350	0		22	
		− 7		2			− 2		2			+ 3		1
360	+ 3		+ 12	+ 2	360	+ 13		+ 12	+ 2	360	+ 3		+ 23	+ 1

TABLE IV.—*Continued.*

PERTURBATIONS OF THE CO-ORDINATES IN UNITS OF THE SIXTII DECIMAL.

	ARGUMENT XV.							ARGUMENT XVI.					
Arg.	ξ'	Diff.	η'	Diff.	ζ'	Diff.	Arg.	ξ'	Diff.	η'	Diff.	ζ'	Diff.
°							°						
0	− 368	−130	−1498	+ 37	− 1		0	+ 196	+ 29	− 347	+ 19	0	
5	498	195	1461	49			5	225	28	328	21		
10	623	121	1412	60	1		10	253	26	307	23		
15	744	115	1352	60			15	279	26	284	25		
20	850	109	1283	69	1		20	303	24	259	25		
25	968	101	1203	80			25	324	21	231	28		
30	1069	94	1114	89	1		30	343	19	202	29		
35	1163	84	1017	97			35	359	16	172	30		
40	1247	84	912	105	− 1		40	373	14	140	32		
45	1322	75	800	112			45	384	11	107	33		
		65		118					6		34		
50	−1387	− 54	− 682	+120	0		50	+ 392	+ 4	− 73	+ 35	0	
55	1441	43	559	128			55	396	+ 2	38	34		
60	1484	32	431	131	0		60	398	− 1	− 4	35		
65	1516	21	300	133			65	397	4	+ 31	34		
70	1537	− 8	167	134	0		70	393	7	65	34		
75	1545	+ 3	− 33	134			75	386	10	99	34		
80	1542	14	+ 101	134	0		80	376	13	133	34		
85	1528	27	235	134			85	363	16	165	32		
90	1501	38	367	122	+ 1		90	347	19	196	31		
95	1463	48	496	129			95	328	21	225	29		
		48		128					21		28		
100	−1415	+ 60	+ 622	+121	+ 1		100	+ 307	− 23	+ 253	+ 26	0	
105	1355	70	743	115			105	284	25	279	24		
110	1285	80	858	108	1		110	259	28	303	21		
115	1205	89	966	101			115	231	29	324	19		
120	1116	98	1067	93	1		120	202	31	343	16		
125	1018	105	1160	85			125	171	32	359	14		
130	913	112	1245	74	1		130	139	32	373	11		
135	801	118	1319	65			135	106	33	384	8		
140	683	124	1384	54	1		140	73	33	392	4		
145	550	127	1438	43			145	38	35	396			
		127		43					35				
150	− 432	+131	+1481	+ 32	+ 2		150	+ 3	− 34	+ 398	+ 2	0	
155	301	134	1513	21			155	− 31	34	397	− 1		
160	167	134	1534	+ 8	2		160	66	35	393	4		
165	− 33	135	1542	− 2			165	100	34	385	8		
170	+ 102	134	1540	15	1		170	133	33	375	10		
175	236	+132	1525	− 27			175	165	32	362	13		
180	+ 368		+1498		+ 1		180	− 196	− 31	+ 347	− 15	0	

From the Arguments > 180° subtract 180°, and reverse the sign of ξ', η', ζ'.

TABLE IV.—*Continued.*

PERTURBATIONS OF THE CO-ORDINATES IN UNITS OF THE SIXTH DECIMAL.

ARGUMENT XVII.

Arg.	ξ'	Diff.	η'	Diff.	ζ'	Diff.
0	− 41	− 14	− 166	+ 4	0	
5	55	14	162	6		
10	69	13	156	6		
15	82	13	150	8		
20	95	12	142	9		
25	107	11	133	10		
30	118	11	123	10		
35	129	9	113	12		
40	138	8	101	12		
45	146	7	89	13		
50	− 153	− 6	− 76	+ 14	0	
55	159	5	62	14		
60	164	4	48	15		
65	168	2	33	14		
70	170	− 1	19	15		
75	171	+ 1	− 4	15		
80	170	1	+ 11	15		
85	169	3	26	14		
90	166	4	40	15		
95	162	5	55	14		
100	− 157	+ 7	+ 69	+ 13	0	
105	150	8	82	13		
110	142	9	95	12		
115	133	9	107	11		
120	124	11	118	10		
125	113	12	128	10		
130	101	12	138	8		
135	89	13	146	7		
140	76	14	153	6		
145	62	14	159	5		
150	− 48	+ 15	+ 164	+ 4	0	
155	33	14	168	2		
160	19	15	170	+ 1		
165	− 4	15	171	− 1		
170	+ 11	15	170	1		
175	26	+ 15	169	3		
180	+ 41		+ 166		0	

ARGUMENT XVIII.

Arg.	ξ'	Diff.	η'	Diff.	ζ'	Diff.
0	+ 40	− 19	− 105	− 5	− 1	
10	21	20	110	− 2		
20	+ 1	19	112	+ 1	1	
30	− 18	19	111	5		
40	37	18	106	8	1	
50	55	16	98	11		
60	71	14	87	14	1	
70	85	12	73	10		
80	97	8	57	17	1	
90	105	5	40	19		
100	− 110	− 2	− 21	+ 20	− 1	
110	112	+ 1	− 1	19		
120	111	5	+ 18	19	0	
130	106	8	37	18		
140	98	11	55	16	0	
150	87	14	71	14		
160	73	16	85	11	0	
170	57	+ 17	96	+ 9		
180	− 40		+ 105		+ 1	

ARGUMENT XIX.

Arg.	ξ'	Diff.	η'	Diff.	ι'	Diff.
0	+ 102	− 12	+ 62	− 17	− 2	
10	90	15	79	14		
20	75	17	93	11	2	
30	58	18	104	8		
40	40	20	112	5	2	
50	+ 20	21	117	− 1		
60	− 1	20	118	+ 3	2	
70	21	20	115	6		
80	41	19	109	9	2	
90	60	17	100	12		
100	− 77	− 14	− 88	+ 15	− 1	
110	91	12	73	18		
120	103	8	55	18	0	
130	111	5	37	20		
140	116	− 2	− 17	21	+ 1	
150	118	+ 2	+ 4	20		
160	116	5	24	20	1	
170	111	+ 9	44	+ 18		
180	− 102		+ 62		+ 2	

From the Arguments > 180° subtract 180°, and reverse the sign of ξ', η', ζ'.

TABLE IV.—*Continued.*

PERTURBATIONS OF THE CO-ORDINATES IN UNITS OF THE SIXTH DECIMAL.

	ARGUMENT XX.							ARGUMENT XXII.					
Arg.	ξ'	Diff.	η'	Diff.	ζ'	Diff.	Arg.	ξ'	Diff.	η	Diff.	ζ'	Diff.
0	+ 22	+ 7	− 42	+ 4	0		0	− 26	− 2	− 18	+ 5	0	
10	29	7	38	6			10	28	− 2	13	5		
20	36	5	32	7			20	30	0	8	5		
30	41	3	25	7			30	30	0	− 3	6		
40	44	3	18	8			40	30	+ 1	+ 3	5		
50	47	+ 1	10	8			50	29	2	8	5		
60	48	0	− 2	8			60	27	3	13	5		
70	48	− 2	+ 6	8			70	24	4	18	5		
80	46	4	14	8			80	20	4	22	4		
90	42	4	22	7			90	16	5	26	4		
100	+ 38	− 6	+ 29	+ 6	0		100	− 11	+ 5	+ 28	+ 2	0	
110	32	7	35	5			110	− 6	6	30	+ 1		
120	25	7	40	4			120	0	5	31	0		
130	18	8	44	2			130	+ 5	5	31	− 1		
140	10	8	46	+ 1			140	10	5	30	2		
150	+ 2	9	47	0			150	15	5	28	2		
160	− 7	8	47	− 2			160	19	4	26	4		
170	15	− 7	45	− 3			170	23	+ 3	22	− 4		
180	− 22		+ 42		0		180	+ 26		+ 18		0	

	ARGUMENT XXI.							ARGUMENT XXIII.					
Arg.	ξ'	Diff.	η'	Diff.	ζ'	Diff.	Arg.	ξ'	Diff.	η'	Diff.	ζ'	Diff.
0	− 13	+ 9	+ 1	− 12	+ 4		0	− 6	+ 12	+ 67	+ 1	0	
10	− 4	9	− 11	13			10	+ 6	12	68	− 2		
20	+ 5	10	24	11	3		20	18	11	66	4		
30	15	9	35	11			30	29	10	62	6		
40	24	8	46	9	+ 1		40	39	9	56	8		
50	32	7	55	8			50	48	8	48	9		
60	39	6	63	5	− 1		60	56	6	39	10		
70	45	5	68	4			70	62	4	29	11		
80	50	3	72	− 1	3		80	66	+ 2	18	11		
90	53	+ 1	73	+ 1			90	68	0	+ 7	12		
100	+ 54	0	− 72	+ 3	− 5		100	+ 68	− 2	− 5	− 12	0	
110	54	− 2	69	5			110	66	4	17	11		
120	52	3	64	7	6		120	62	6	28	10		
130	49	5	57	9			130	56	8	38	9		
140	44	6	48	10	6		140	48	9	47	8		
150	38	8	38	12			150	39	11	55	6		
160	30	8	26	12	5		160	28	11	61	4		
170	22	− 9	14	+ 13			170	17	− 11	65	− 2		
180	+ 13		− 1		− 4		180	+ 6		− 67		0	

From the Arguments > 180° subtract 180°, and reverse the sign of ξ', η', ζ'.

TABLE IV.—*Concluded.*

PERTURBATIONS OF THE CO-ORDINATES IN UNITS OF THE SIXTH DECIMAL.

ARGUMENT XXIV.				ARGUMENT XXVII.				ARGUMENT XXX.			
Arg.	ξ'	η'	ζ'	Arg.	ξ'	η'	ζ'	Arg.	ξ'	η'	ζ'
0	+ 17	− 20	− 1	0	+ 1	+ 17	0	0	− 5	− 6	0
20	18	24	2	20	7	15		20	− 7	4	
40	17	26	3	40	12	12		40	8	− 1	
60	14	25	3	60	15	7		60	8	+ 2	
80	10	20	4	80	17	+ 2		80	7	4	
100	+ 4	13	3	100	16	− 4		100	5	6	
120	− 2	− 5	2	120	14	9		120	− 3	8	
140	8	+ 4	− 1	140	10	14		140	0	8	
160	13	13	0	160	+ 5	16		160	+ 3	7	
180	− 17	+ 20	+ 1	180	− 1	+ 17	0	180	+ 5	+ 6	0

ARGUMENT XXV.				ARGUMENT XXVIII.			
Arg.	ξ'	η'	ζ'	Arg.	ξ'	η	ζ'
0	+ 5	+ 5	+ 1	0	− 4	− 10	0
20	11	8	1	20	0	11	
40	15	9	1	40	+ 3	10	
60	17	9	+ 1	60	7	8	
80	17	8	0	80	9	6	
100	15	6	0	100	11	− 2	
120	12	4	− 1	120	11	+ 2	
140	7	+ 1	1	140	9	5	
160	+ 1	− 3	1	160	7	8	
180	− 5	− 5	− 1	180	+ 4	+ 10	0

ARGUMENT XXVI.				ARGUMENT XXIX.			
Arg.	ξ'	η'	ζ	Arg.	ξ'	η'	ζ'
0	− 1	− 23	0	0	− 5	+ 8	0
20	9	21		20	7	6	
40	15	17		40	9	+ 3	
60	20	11		60	9	0	
80	23	− 3		80	8	− 3	
100	22	+ 5		100	7	6	
120	19	12		120	4	8	
140	14	18		140	− 1	9	
160	− 7	22		160	+ 2	9	
180	+ 1	+ 23	0	180	+ 5	− 8	0

From the Arguments > 180° subtract 180°, and reverse the sign of ξ', η', ζ'.

TABLE V.

LOGARITHMS FOR REFERRING THE PERTURBATIONS TO THE EQUATOR.

Mean Equinox of the beginning of the Year.

Year.	$\cos(x_1 x)$	$\cos(y_1 x)$	$\cos(z_1 x)$	$\cos(x_1 y)$	$\cos(y_1 y)$	$\cos(z_1 y)$	$\cos(x_1 z)$	$\cos(y_1 z)$	$\cos(z_1 z)$
1850	9.862239	9.833908	8.820053	9.793764n	9.844007	9.549470n	9.459233n	9.336366	9.969772
1851	9.862338	9.833796	8.819976	9.793671n	9.844102	9.549452n	9.459126n	9.336499	9.969774
1852 B	9.862437	9.833683	8.819899	9.793557n	9.844196	9.549434n	9.459020n	9.336631	9.969777
1853	9.862536	9.833571	8.819823	9.793444n	9.844290	9.549416n	9.458913n	9.336764	9.969780
1854	9.862635	9.833458	8.819746	9.793330n	9.844384	9.549398n	9.458806n	9.336896	9.969783
1855	9.862734	9.833346	8.819669	9.793217n	9.844479	9.549380n	9.458700n	9.337029	9.969786
1856 B	9.862833	9.833233	8.819592	9.793103n	9.844573	9.549362n	9.458593n	9.337161	9.969789
1857	9.862932	9.833120	8.819515	9.792990n	9.844667	9.549344n	9.458486n	9.337293	9.969792
1858	9.863031	9.833007	8.819438	9.792876n	9.844761	9.549326n	9.458379n	9.337425	9.969795
1859	9.863130	9.832896	8.819362	9.792763n	9.844855	9.549308n	9.458272n	9.337557	9.969798
1860 B	9.863229	9.832781	8.819285	9.792649n	9.844949	9.549290n	9.458165n	9.337689	9.969801
1861	9.863328	9.832668	8.819208	9.792535n	9.845043	9.519272n	9.458059n	9.337821	9.969804
1862	9.863426	9.832555	8.819131	9.792421n	9.845137	9.519254n	9.457951n	9.337952	9.969807
1863	9.863525	9.832442	8.819054	9.792307n	9.845231	9.549236n	9.457844n	9.338084	9.969810
1864 B	9.863624	9.832329	8.818977	9.792193n	9.845325	9.549218n	9.457737n	9.338216	9.969813
1865	9.863722	9.832216	8.818900	9.792079n	9.845419	9.549200n	9.457630n	9.338348	9.969816
1866	9.863820	9.832103	8.818823	9.791905n	9.845512	9.549183n	9.457592n	9.338479	9.969819
1867	9.863918	9.831990	8.818747	9.791851n	9.845606	9.549162n	9.457415n	9.338611	9.969822
1868 B	9.864016	9.831876	8.818670	9.791737n	9.845700	9.549142n	9.457307n	9.338742	9.969825
1869	9.864114	9.831763	8.818593	9.791623n	9.845794	9.549126n	9.457200n	9.338873	9.969828
1870	9.864213	9.831649	8.818516	9.791508n	9.845887	9.549111n	9.457092n	9.339004	9.969831
1871	9.864311	9.831536	8.818440	9.791393n	9.845981	9.549093n	9.456985n	9.339135	9.969834
1872 B	9.864409	9.831422	8.818363	9.791279n	9.846074	9.549075n	9.456877n	9.339266	9.969837
1873	9.864507	9.831309	8.818286	9.791165n	9.846168	9.549057n	9.456769n	9.339397	9.969840
1874	9.864606	9.831195	8.818209	9.791050n	9.846261	9.549039n	9.456661n	9.339527	9.969843
1875	9.864704	9.831081	8.818133	9.790936n	9.846355	9.549021n	9.156553n	9.339658	9.969846
1876 B	9.864802	9.830967	8.818056	9.790821n	9.846448	9.549003n	9.456445n	9.339788	9.969849
1877	9.864900	9.830853	8.817979	9.790706n	9.846541	9.548985n	9.456337n	9.339919	9.969852
1878	9.864999	9.830739	8.817902	9.790591n	9.846634	9.548967n	9.456229n	9.340049	9.969855
1879	9.865097	9.830625	8.817825	9.790477n	9.846728	9.548949n	9.456121n	9.340180	9.969858
1880 B	9.865195	9.830511	8.817748	9.790362n	9.846921	9.548931n	9.456013n	9.340310	9.969861
1881	9.865293	9.830397	8.817672	9.790247n	9.846914	9.548913n	9.455905n	9.340440	9.969864
1882	9.865390	9.830283	8.817595	9.790132n	9.847007	9.548896n	9.455797n	9.340570	9.969867
1883	9.865487	9.830169	8.817517	9.790017n	9.847100	9.548878n	9.455689n	9.340700	9.969869
1884 B	9.865585	9.830055	8.817440	9.789902n	9.847193	9.548860n	9.455581n	9.340830	9.969872
1885	9.865682	9.829941	8.817363	9.789787n	9.847286	9.548842n	9.455473n	9.340960	9.969875
1886	9.865780	9.829896	8.817285	9.789672n	9.847379	9.548825n	9.455364n	9.341090	9.969878
1887	9.865877	9.829712	8.817208	9.789557n	9.847472	9.548807n	9.455256n	9.341220	9.969881
1888 B	9.865975	9.829597	8.817130	9.789442n	9.847565	9.548789n	9.455148n	9.341350	9.969884
1889	9.866072	9.829483	8.817053	9.789327n	9.847658	9.548771n	9.455040n	9.341480	9.969887
1890	9.866170	9.829368	8.816975	9.789211n	9.847750	9.548754n	9.454931n	9.341609	9.969890
1891	9.866267	9.829253	8.816898	9.789096n	9.847843	9.548736n	9.454823n	9.341739	9.969893
1892 B	9.866365	9.829139	8.816820	9.788980n	9.847935	9.548718n	9.454714n	9.341869	9.969896
1893	9.866462	9.829025	8.816743	9.788865n	9.848028	9.548700n	9.454606n	9.341998	9.969899
1894	9.866559	9.828910	8.816665	9.788749n	9.848120	9.548683n	9.454497n	9.342127	9.969902
1895	9.866650	9.828796	8.816588	9.788634n	9.848213	9.548665n	9.454389n	9.342257	9.969905
1896 B	9.866754	9.828681	8.816510	9.788518n	9.848305	9.548647n	9.454280n	9.342386	9.969908
1897	9.866851	9.828566	8.816433	9.788402n	9.848398	9.548629n	9.454172n	9.342515	9.969911
1898	9.866948	9.828451	8.816355	9.788286n	9.848490	9.548612n	9.454063n	9.342644	9.969914
1899	9.867045	9.828336	8.816278	9.788170n	9.848583	9.548594n	9.453958n	9.342774	9.969917
1900 B	9.867143	9.828221	8.816200	9.788054n	9.848675	9.548576n	9.453849n	9.342903	9.969920

TABLE VI.

CONSTANTS FOR THE EQUATOR.

Equator and mean Equinox at the beginning of the Year.

Year.	A'	B'	C'	log sin a	log sin b	log sin c
	° ′ ″	° ′ ″	° ′ ″			
1850	46 52 2.4	318 18 19.9	307 0 4.4	9.999051	9.970859	9.556901
1851	46 52 52.5	318 19 8.8	307 0 58.9	9.999051	9.970861	9.556871
1852 B	46 53 42.8	318 19 57.9	307 1 53.6	9.999051	9.970864	9.556851
1853	46 54 33.0	318 20 46.8	307 2 48.1	9.999052	9.970866	9.556831
1854	46 55 23.1	318 21 35.8	307 3 42.7	9.999052	9.970869	9.556811
1855	46 56 13.2	318 21 24.7	307 4 37.2	9.999052	9.970871	9.556791
1856 B	46 57 3.5	318 23 13.8	307 5 31.9	9.999053	9.970874	9.556771
1857	46 57 53.7	318 24 2.7	307 6 26.5	9.999053	9.970876	9.556751
1858	46 58 43.8	318 24 51.7	307 7 21.0	9.999053	9.970879	9.556731
1859	46 59 34.0	318 25 40.6	307 8 15.6	9.999053	9.970881	9.556711
1860 B	47 0 24.2	318 26 29.7	307 9 10.3	9.999053	9.970884	9.556691
1861	47 1 14.4	318 27 18.6	307 10 4.8	9.999054	9.970886	9.556671
1862	47 2 4.5	318 28 7.6	307 10 59.4	9.999054	9.970889	9.556651
1863	47 2 54.6	318 28 56.5	307 11 54.0	9.999054	9.970891	9.556631
1864 B	47 3 44.9	318 29 45.6	307 12 48.7	9.999054	9.970894	9.556611
1865	47 4 35.0	318 30 34.6	307 13 43.3	9.999055	9.970897	9.556591
1866	47 5 25.2	318 31 23.5	307 14 37.9	9.999055	9.970900	9.556572
1867	47 6 17.3	318 32 12.4	307 15 32.5	9.999055	9.970902	9.556552
1868 B	47 7 7.6	318 33 1.5	307 16 27.2	9.999055	9.970905	9.556532
1869	47 7 57.7	318 33 50.5	307 17 21.8	9.999056	9.970908	9.556512
1870	47 8 45.9	318 34 39.4	307 18 16.4	9.999056	9.970910	9.556492
1871	47 9 26.0	318 25 29.4	307 19 11.0	9.999056	9.970912	9.556472
1872 B	47 10 26.2	318 36 17.5	307 20 5.8	9.999056	9.970915	9.556452
1873	47 11 16.4	318 37 6.4	307 21 0.4	9.999057	9.970917	9.556432
1874	47 12 6.5	318 37 55.4	307 21 55.0	9.999057	9.970920	9.556413
1875	47 12 56.6	318 38 44.4	307 22 49.6	9.999057	9.970922	9.556393
1876 B	47 13 46.9	318 39 33.5	307 23 44.3	9.999057	9.970925	9.556373
1877	47 14 37.0	318 40 22.4	307 24 39.0	9.999058	9.970928	9.556353
1878	47 15 27.2	318 41 11.4	307 25 33.6	9.999058	9.970930	9.556333
1879	47 16 17.3	318 42 0.4	307 26 18.2	9.999058	9.970933	9.556313
1880 B	47 17 7.5	318 42 49.4	307 27 12.9	9.999059	9.970935	9.556293
1881	47 17 57.7	318 43 38.4	307 28 7.5	9.999059	9.970938	9.556273
1882	47 18 47.8	318 44 27.4	307 29 12.2	9.999060	9.970941	9.556254
1883	47 19 37.9	318 45 16.4	307 30 6.8	9.999060	9.970943	9.556234
1884 B	47 20 28.2	318 46 5.5	307 31 1.6	9.999060	9.970946	9.556214
1885	47 21 18.3	318 46 54.4	307 31 56.2	9.999061	9.970948	9.556194
1886	47 22 8.4	318 47 43.4	307 32 50.9	9.999061	9.970951	9.556175
1887	47 22 58.5	318 48 32.4	307 33 45.5	9.999061	9.970953	9.556155
1888 B	47 23 48.8	318 49 21.5	307 34 40.3	9.999062	9.970956	9.556135
1889	47 24 38.9	318 50 10.5	307 35 34.9	9.999062	9.970958	9.556115
1890	47 25 29.0	318 50 59.5	307 36 29.5	9.999063	9.970961	9.556096
1891	47 26 19.1	318 51 48.4	307 37 24.2	9.999063	9.970963	9.556076
1892 B	47 27 9.4	318 52 37.5	307 38 19.0	9.999064	9.970966	9.556056
1893	47 27 59.5	318 53 26.5	307 39 13.6	9.999064	9.970968	9.556036
1894	47 28 49.6	318 54 15.5	307 40 8.3	9.999065	9.970971	9.556017
1895	47 29 39.7	318 55 4.5	307 41 2.9	9.999065	9.970974	9.555997
1896 B	47 30 30.0	318 55 53.6	307 41 57.7	9.999066	9.970976	9.555977
1897	47 31 20.1	318 56 42.6	307 42 51.3	9.999066	9.970979	9.555957
1898	47 32 10.2	318 57 31.6	307 43 47.0	9.999067	9.970982	9.555938
1899	47 33 0.3	318 58 20.6	307 44 41.6	9.999067	9.970985	9.555918
1900 B	47 33 50.5	318 59 9.7	307 45 36.4	9.999068	9.970987	9.555898

www.ingramcontent.com/pod-product-compliance
Lightning Source LLC
Chambersburg PA
CBHW022042080426
42733CB00007B/937